CHAPPED
LEGS AND
PUNCTURED
BALLS

CHAPPED LEGS AND PUNCTURED BALLS

Paul Cooper

SPORTS
BOOKS

Published in Great Britain by
SportsBooks Limited
PO Box 422
Cheltenham
GL50 2YN
United Kingdom

Tel: 01242 256755
Fax: 0560 3108126
email: info@sportsbooks.ltd.uk
www.sportsbooks.ltd.uk

First published November 2009

A catalogue record for this book is available from
the British Library.

Cover drawing by Aczel

ISBN 978 1899807 87 1

Printed and bound by Thomson Litho Ltd,
East Kilbride, Scotland

INTRODUCTION

The World Cup wasn't won (in 1966) on the playing fields of England. It was won on the streets.
Bobby Charlton

North Devon is not exactly a hotbed of football.

I grew up there in the 1960s before the M4, M5 and the Atlantic Highway were built – the latter is not a heavy metal album but the tourist board's glitzy name for the A39 from Tiverton to Bideford.

Back then it would take six weeks to get to London on the back of a sheepdog and because this part of the world was fairly remote it meant there was very little organised football for the kids.

If you want to know what it was like living there in the 1960s, pop down to north Devon now – it's exactly the same. The Beatles are always at number one and *The Sound of Music* is showing at the Strand cinema.

There is a road block on the A39, sorry Atlantic Highway, where they make you park up your 4x4 and other such modern models and loan you the choice of a Ford Anglia or Morris Minor for the weekend. They throw in a tartan rug and a thermos of Camp coffee for good measure. If you are very lucky you may even find a packet of Spangles in the glove compartment.

I am from the generation that played out. Remember those days? When you stepped outside, climbed trees, rode bikes, explored, built dens, threw stones at cats, played football, cricket, and climbed Everest in nothing more than a light windcheater and shorts with a cheese and pickle sandwich in one pocket and a rolled up copy of last week's *Beano* in the other. All this and you would still be home in time for tea.

The sun shone every day and it was always the summer holidays.

It may appear to the reader that I look back at childhood through rose-coloured spectacles, but there were bad days and some very dark times that have been pushed to the back of my brain and only surface in times of great stress, such as when I can't find the remote control for the TV.

The darkest memory has to be one dreadful Christmas when I wrote to Santa asking for a Scalectrix, but got a watch instead. I was haunted by this childhood trauma for years and thought I had found the solution when I included a Scalectrix on our wedding list and got matching his and her watches and comments like, 'what a character' at the reception.

For my fiftieth birthday I played cute and employed reverse psychology by end-lessly asking for a watch which duly arrived on the day, beautifully engraved. 'We were going to get you a Scalectrix,' my wife informed me, 'but you seemed so insistent on having yet another watch that we got you that instead.'

There were some big events in the sixties. Where were you when the first man landed on the moon? Or when Kennedy was assassinated? I'll always remember the latter moment, more for the reaction of my father. My brother was at brass band practice and dad said, 'I must go and pick him up straight away. He will be devastated.'

I was never quite sure what the connection was between the president of the United States and a ten-year-old cornet player from north Devon.

For ages I had this picture in my mind of my brother coming out of the hall with his cornet tucked under his arm and my father saying, 'Kennedy's been shot dead'.

My brother responding by running towards him shaking his head and crying, 'No No No!'

One of the main things etched on my memory also came in the sixties and to this day I still have chills down my spine remembering it.

I had saved three weeks' pocket money to buy the Beatles' single *From Me to You*. My mother went into town and was going to buy the record on her way home. I was watching the football results on *Grandstand* when I heard the front door open and dashed excitedly into the hall. I knew something was up from the expression on mum's face as she explained that they had sold out of the Beatles single but not to worry she had bought me Mike Sarne's record *Will I What?* featuring a cameo performance by Wendy Richards of *Are You Being Served* and *Eastenders* fame. Gutted!

I hated school, except for the football in the playground, and those long summer holidays which inevitably came to an end. To keep my mind off doomsday I would throw myself into six new hobbies in the last three days – Russian coins, Pike fishing, building Airfix World War Two kits, stick whittling and stamp collecting would be a typical mixture.

Hopefully the rest of my time on this earth will also be like those long summer holidays. However, recently I have thought about buying a shed and sitting in it wearing nothing more than a bottle green coloured cardigan and having a ball of twine in one pocket and a packet of radish seeds in the other.

I have also become strangely attracted to first day covers, books on Austrian dairy farming, collecting vintage roof racks, crown green bowls and underwater yoga.

I am trying to figure out if this is nature's gentle way of saying I have an incurable disease and have just three days to live or that I am mentally unstable?

EQUIPMENT

I was football mad as a boy. In that big back garden I'd kick a tennis ball around for hours. Along with the other boys from Ivy House Road we'd play football in the street with the tennis ball until it was bald. Even when the bald tennis ball split we still played football with it. When the tennis ball finally gave up the ghost that didn't stop us either. I had countless kickabouts in the street with half a tennis ball.
Jimmy Greaves

BALLS

The Leather Football

The old leather football had a bladder inside an outer leather casing. Part of the ball was laced, so as to gain access to the bladder.

When brand spanking new the ball was fine, if a little heavy. However, no material known to man changes as much, under the influence of water, as the leather they used for old-fashioned footballs.

When carelessly left out in the garden at night in the rain it turned into a killing machine. The same effect could also be produced by leaving it out in a heavy frost. The heaviness of the ball went from the FA regulation weight to twice the weight of a baby elephant.

The other hazard was the lacing, which if headed in a particular place could open up the forehead deeper than a Hussar's sabre.

The Light Plastic Ball

Cheap ball that came in a cheap plastic net. Usually red, yellow or blue with black hexagons.

The ball was so light that even the slightest breeze could waft it to Venezuela and beyond.

Frowned on by all street footballers and usually only purchased by well meaning grandparents existing on a small state pension. The remedy was a quick kick about in Granddad's garden and a volley into the nearest rose bush. The punctured version of the 'light plastic ball' was actually better for street football but was a bugger to head.

The Slightly Heavier Plastic Ball

This slightly more expensive ball was usually white with black hexagons, and the names of First Division teams printed on it. A version with pictures of the Beatles was also available in the mid-sixties.

Unlike the cheaper, light, version, it came with a small adaptor with which to pump it up. Like its cheaper cousin it was prone to puncture. When the ball was travelling towards a rose bush or anything spikey, many street footballers experienced a kind of strange spasm that would take hold of the whole body in the couple of seconds that would determine if the ball was punctured or not.

Many hours were wasted trying to repair these punctured footballs. First spittle was applied to the area thought to be punctured. After the tell-tale bubbling signs, the area was dried and, depending on your degree of intelligence, the following would be applied.

The very dim would affix an elastoplast (the advert tells you that it is a breathable bandage which you would think would give the game away). The slightly less dim would use a bicycle tyre puncture repair kit, which was about as useful on plastic footballs as it was on bicycle tyres.

The clever street footballers and smokers would use a lit match to melt a small area of the ball at the puncture site and scrape molten plastic over the hole. This was only ever a temporary measure as the ball would still lose air and become too much of a chore to pump up every five minutes.

This ball was an evil chunk of plastic if played with when punctured, unlike its cheaper copy.

The Wembley Trophy Ball

The Holy Grail of street football.

The successor to the Frido, the ball was quite expensive, so was usually given only as Christmas or birthday presents. Orange with black lines, it came in a square presentation box with panels cut out to show the sexy curves of the ball. The box boasted that the ball was regulation weight, the same as the more expensive leather ball.

Street football was great in the couple of months post-Christmas because of the abundance of Wembley Trophies, but by the following December most Wembley Trophies had been punctured, lost or stolen. Having one of these balls punctured was like losing a favourite family pet.

You had to beware the cheap imitation ball sold at Woolworths under their own Winfield brand label.

Any street footballer who had a Wembley Trophy down on his Christmas list and received one of the Winfields instead would cry under the bed covers at night for weeks.

He would rather play with his little sister's Sindy dolls than that fake pretender.

The Tennis Ball

Much loved by all street footballers and the main ball of choice for playground football. This ball could be stowed away in trouser pockets and was cheap and plentiful. It did not burst but would, like a middle-aged man, eventually lose all its hair and morph into a rubber ball which eventually split along the seam. Not that a middle-aged man does that last bit.

This was the ball used by the great stars of the past like Matthews, Finney and Charlton and was often kicked against a wall.

The emergence of the larger plastic football in place of the tennis ball was seen as the beginning of the end for 'good ball players' in this country.

In those days everybody wanted to be a footballer and play for his local team. I used to practise often against a wall with a tennis ball, not a big ball because we couldn't afford it in those days. And because it was a small ball it improved my ball control.
Stanley Matthews

The Airflow Ball

Hated and despised by street footballers. Indeed, playground footballers would often prefer to use a stone in place of this useless piece of plastic.

The airflow ball got its name because it was dotted with holes, held together by rigid, shiny plastic, so that the ball would go just a short distance. Made for golfers to practise in the garden and the size of a proper golf ball. Also sold in pet shops with the addition of a bell inside for the amusement of bored cats.

Would last for just a few minutes in the hurly-burly of the playground arena before someone stepped on it and the pathetic object was crushed into a dozen pieces.

The Rubber Ball

The same size as a tennis ball and bought by poverty stricken street footballers who could not afford to buy its more illustrious cousin. Usually orange, but occasionally blue.

Also sold in pet shops for the amusement of dogs that salivated a lot.

The Stone

Used in the playground as a last resort and occasionally headed by the class lunatic.

The Baby's Ball

Soft furry and with a bell inside; this was a joy to play with indoors.

The favourite game was throwing the ball up for diving headers. Although soft the ball could travel and was responsible for countless smacked arses in our house after it had smashed many a family heirloom.

The Balloon

A good ball substitute on a very wet day indoors. The balloon was headed, chested and hit with the thigh; however, it rarely had time to get down to the feet. The goals were normally open doors; the hallway was a favourite arena.

The only drawback with balloon football was if you were short. The game was nearly always won by the tallest player, who could run with the balloon balanced on his forehead into the goal.

Often that was the only way older brothers, who were crap at football, could win a game. That is why they can do a pretty mean rain dance.

Also strong players could score by gripping the ball between their knees and hopping towards the goal, elbowing anything and anyone within a six foot radius. This was deemed not very skilful but incredibly effective.

The Beach Ball

B-l-o-o-d-y u-s-e-l-e-s-s

FOOTWEAR

Football Boots

Not often worn by the street footballer unless you had a match against another team or gang down the park.

The *coup de grace* was the George Best, maroon, side lace-up boots. Cooler than a chopper bike and nearly as expensive. Out of the reach of most kids who had to settle for 'school football boots' own brand from Freeman Hardy & Willis.

About as cool as wearing your granddad's orthopaedic shoe and about as effective.

Plimsolls/Gym shoes

In the sixties the only 'trainers' were men who sat next to the manager on the bench with a towel around their neck. They would run onto the pitch from time to time with a metal bucket filled with ice-cold water and a large sponge.

The plimsoll was used a lot by street footballers, not because they were seen as trendy, but because everybody had to have a pair for school.

The Dap

The cheap man's plimsoll was black, elasticated and excellent for street football. It did have a stigma as some of the poorer kids at school wore nothing else, rain, snow or sunshine. It felt like playing in slippers but gave very little protection from heavy challenges.

The elastic left a strange mosaic pattern on the top of the foot similar to the Gaelic band tattoos worn around the top of the arm by dodgy girls and geezers in the late nineties.

The dap was the ballet shoe of street football.

The Basket Ball Boot

Very trendy but not ideal for street football as the big rubber toe-cap and surround gave a poor feel for the ball.

Sneakers

Another American influence, and similar to the gym shoe in that it was canvas based. An assortment of colours and different shaped toes made them cool but they did split fairly easily at the front.

School Shoes

Always black, these took a hell of a battering in the playground and were the biggest area of discord between a child and parent.

No matter what footwear you had in your gym bag, you would never dream of wearing anything other than your school shoes for playing footie in the playground.

The most often used phrase by an adult in the sixties, while looking down at a pair of brand new but scuffed school shoes, was 'why don't you put your daps on when you play football.'

The standard, lace-up variety were worn only by boring kids with glasses, who looked like bank managers even at the tender age of ten.

Then there was the slip-on which was quite trendy but one of the most dangerous weapons known to man, ranking somewhere between the Scud missile and the Atom bomb. Many a goalkeeper has been dragged from his goal to the school nurses' room after being hit by an Exocet Clarks' slip-on.

This scenario was played out on playgrounds around the country until the slip-on became less trendy.

A player through on goal hits a volley with all his might. He mistimes the shot and his slip-on travels faster than the speed of sound, striking the hapless goalie on the forehead and knocking him backwards and unconscious into his goal. The mishit ball meanwhile trickles innocuously over the line.

In fact, some weak players purposefully got their mums to buy them slip-ons, and a size too big to boot, so they flew off the foot at the players' will.

This gave them a certain street cred in the playground with regard to how many goalies they had permanently disfigured.

When the slip-on was at the height of fashion, the sky over the playground would become dark with the number of these shoes in the air. Dinner ladies and teachers likened it to the blitz.

The Chelsea Boot

The king of the school shoe and even cool enough to wear outside school was the Chelsea Boot. These had a zip at the side, and bright red or blue lining. The heel could be quite large which made them difficult to play in but great for defending set pieces.

The boot length could be anything from just covering the ankle to reaching well up the thigh.

The boys loved them, the girls loved to see the boys in them and everyone was happy except for exasperated parents as these passion clogs were much more expensive than the boring lace-up variety.

School shoes were rarely polished and with all the running about playing football in the playground they used to sag around the ankle and looked as if you had the gout-plagued lower leg of an obese 18th century aristocrat.

Slippers

In the days before Super Ted, Superman and Tin Tin, we had a choice between burgundy, navy blue or, for the more grown up, checked slippers.

Slippers were worn for bedroom and hallway football, and occasionally outside by lazy street footballers who could not be bothered to change and were prepared to have a larger, size ten slipper, making contact several times with their derrière on their return home.

Desert Boots

Excellent for chasing Field Marshall Erwin Rommel around North Africa, but if worn now would be responsible for many meta-tarsal injuries (Break it like Beckham) as the boot crumples on impact.

I had a pair of desert boots and was made to wear them on formal occasions as an alternative to school shoes. As my brother and father also wore them, on family outings we looked like the cast of *Daktari*. We only needed to camouflage the family Allegro and own a cross-eyed lion to make the deception complete.

Wellingtons

I wore Wellies only once when playing football. It was like playing with a couple of coffins strapped to your legs.

I had been fishing with my mates. In the thirteen years I lived in north Devon and fished in the River Torridge I never caught a fish. But I bagged millions of crabs, which we threw at each other and craftily popped into one another's duffle coat hood.

CLOTHING

Duffle Coats

These were very popular for a time in the sixties. On a cold day everyone would turn up in a duffle coat, so to distinguish the two teams, one side wore their hoods up and the other side wore them down.

For the casual observer it looked like some obscure sect of Belgian Trappist monks who brew their own wheat beer for sale in expensive supermarkets.

When it rained, the steam coming from thirty or so duffle coats was enough to turn the pitch into a re-creation of Jack the Ripper's, smog-filled London.

By the end of a game the temperature inside a duffle coat reached levels hotter than the sun. It was not uncommon for a winger, running down the flank at full pace, to self combust.

The Windcheater

The really trendy version had a tartan lining and was called a Harrington. While researching this book I was rather disappointed to find out that it had been named after the jacket worn by Rodney Harrington, played by Ryan O'Neal in the TV series *Peyton Place*. No respecting street footballer would be seen dead watching the programme, as it was a boring soap, strictly for mums. However the Harrington was dead cool.

There were also many cheaper copies, one of which I owned. I further lowered my street footballer cred by getting my mum to sew cloth badges on the sleeve. I had Portland Lighthouse, Weymouth, Clovelly, Weston-super-Mare, London (a soldier wearing a Busby in a sentry box outside Buckingham Palace) the New Forest and St Tropez.

The School Jumper

The grey school jumper was sometimes worn on cold days as everyone had one. The only time it had any use was when playing either Richard the Lionheart, Ivanhoe or Robin Hood. When we pulled the jumper up at the back and stretched it over our head, we thought it looked like chainmail. If the jumper was on the small side it meant that your sword and shield arm could hardly move and you became easy prey for the Sheriff of Nottingham's henchmen.

Matching Jumpers

The nightmare scenario for brothers. Indeed you sometimes wished you were an only child and even go without having a football partner rather than endure this humiliation.

On special occasions when our family were visiting people who were richer than us, my father made my brother and I wear a hideous pair of matching jumpers. They were navy blue and across the chest had a ridiculous pattern, which was of a winter scene with snowflakes and some kind of animal from northern climes charging across a wooded landscape.

It is the kind of garment that a spiv from Lapland would sell to American tourists, but would never dream of making their own children wear it.

I can't imagine what my parents were thinking of?

The typical scenario would be going for pre Sunday lunch drinks at the home of someone my dad wanted to impress.

What did he think our snotty-nosed host would say to his even snottier-nosed wife?

'They may be considerably poorer than us, but they show remarkable class and style, dressing their boys in those very fetching jumpers.'

The other humiliation was that we were made to 'play' with the hosts' children who always went to boarding school, looked down at my brother and me, and sneered at our matching jumpers.

The day usually ended in my brother whacking one of them and severe embarrassment for our parents.

If my dad ever came downstairs wearing a cravat, you knew it was a matching jumpers day.

School Blazer

It is difficult to find anything more cringe worthy to wear than matching jumpers, but the school blazer managed it. If our father thought the occasion even more special, the school uniform came out. Nowadays kids wear a school sweatshirt, but back then it was blazer, short trousers, tie and cap.

What a hideous way to walk around. It was bad enough wearing the dreadful ensemble for school, but outside it brought acute embarrassment into a new category.

Our dad, again, made my brother and I wear our school uniforms to weddings, important family gatherings and to the 1968 Spurs v Sunderland match.

I was ecstatic when I heard that we were going up to stay with my granddad in London and that he was going to take my brother and me to our first proper professional football match.

Up until then I had only watched Bideford FC and thought that Peter Druce was better than Pele.

But our joy of going to the game was tempered by the announcement that we were going to be the only two people in a crowd of thirty-thousand, wearing our school uniforms.

On the train from Liverpool Street station, granddad and my brother and I were in a compartment with a gang of skinheads. I didn't know what they were as this youth cult would not reach north Devon for another ten years, and then there was only one.

They kept nudging each other and sniggering at our dress. I couldn't help noticing that they were wearing big lace-up boots and I thought that was really naff. Slip-on shoes were all the rage in Bideford and I kept sticking out my thin, pale, leg with a Clarks' black slip-on dangling at the end. I kept trying to catch their attention, and when I did, I nodded down to my slip-on to try and claw back some street cred and they all nudged each other and burst into hysterical laughter.

No one can ever prepare you for that first time you walk up the steps of a football ground, and emerge into the stand and glimpse the green of the pitch below. I was in heaven, and that memory will stay with me for ever.

The game was great and we saw Jimmy Greaves score four goals. I was so full of the experience I could have been dressed in just a tutu for all I cared on the train journey back into central London.

Snake Belts

Not quite as exciting as the name suggests. They are not made from adder skin but take their name from the snake-shaped clasp.

The belts were usually two different colours, yellow and navy blue, red and black and other such colourful combinations.

They kept up your grey shorts in primary school while you played football in the playground and kept your long grey trousers up at secondary school as you also played football in the playground, in addition to setting fire to the bike shed.

The character, Ranji Ram from the TV comedy *It Ain't Half Hot Mum* even wore one to keep his turban in place.

These belts were elasticated and had other uses. In primary school a group of us playing a game of Medieval Sieges had, in just ten minutes, produced a siege machine from half a dozen snake belts, the caretaker's broom and a Wembley Trophy football. It was capable of knocking down the walls of Jericho.

We managed to break the staffroom window but it was easy for the teachers to spot the perpetrators as they all had their school shorts around their ankles.

It never ceased to amaze me, the number of people who had trouble adjusting the size of their snake belt. On the side was a simple buckle device to lengthen or shorten the belt. Yet I saw so many people suffer, with the tops of their trousers looking like potato sacks.

The strength of the snake belt had the power to stop the entire blood circulation travelling south. When you saw a boy with legs the circumference of two white cotton threads and swaying from side to side, the clues were obvious. A quick adjustment at the side of the belt and his legs went back to the normal size and colour within minutes. 'Oh, so that's what that thing at the side is for!'

Gloves

Keepers rarely wore gloves before the seventies, apart from some foreigners, but we sometimes wore them in goal if it was snowing. They were made of wool and when waterlogged weighed your arms down so much that you had to save the ball with your feet.

A few years later I went on to play in goal for the factory team and through not wearing gloves received some bad finger injuries, leaving them pointing in various directions. I am now one of a selective band of people that can both play the piano and pick my nose at the same time.

I was given the nickname 'The Cat', but not so much for my springy athletic diving ability but because of my rather dodgy nocturnal activities.

VENUES

From a technical standpoint, I couldn't help but improve my skills. Anybody can trap and control a ball on a picture-perfect billiard table smooth pitch. But where I played, you had to learn how to control the ball no matter what, regardless of whether it bounced off the rubbish or skidded along the gutter. I learned how to dribble up steps, how to run non-stop for hours (there was no such thing as 'out of bounds') and how to thread my way through tight spaces (we played eleven-a-side on a pitch which would have been tight for a five-a-side). I guess much of my close control and dribbling ability originated on the Stenditoi.
Paolo Di Canio

When we talk about street football it is football played in the street, in the parks, on waste ground, and in the school playground. It was really any football where adults were not involved, from a time where their only involvement was a call from your Mum to come in for tea.

This was the children's game.

The Street

The street could be a lane, a dual carriageway, cul-de-sac or a path. It really depended on where you lived and if your Dad had plenty of dosh. The more dosh, the fewer players. The middle classes generally frowned on street football and thought the boys should be helping old people with their gardens, playing chess, or constructing a posh, detached, 1930s-style suburban house from Meccano.

The other thing middle-class parents longed for was for their children to invent a wonder drug with their 17s 6d chemistry sets at the kitchen table. Sadly, like street football, the chemistry set has all but disappeared. Today's mixed-up, middle-class teenagers, far from trying to save the world with a new cure, as their parents had done before them, are more inclined, given a chemistry set, either to make hallucinogenic drugs or produce homemade bombs to blow up people in white coats who do nasty things to fluffy bunny rabbits.

The other hazard was the middle-class garden which was full of tall flowers just waiting to be knocked over. The misery of footie mad middle-class kids was intolerable, as from an early age they realised that they were destined to work in an office or a bank. They may have taken some comfort that they would pass their eleven-plus and go to grammar school, but in their hearts they knew the nearest they would get to playing at Wembley was with the Bishop Auckland Subbuteo team in the Amateur Cup played out on the dining table.

Real street football was played on the estates and outside the rows of terraced houses, all day by hundreds of kids. This was the breeding ground of generation after generation of great ball players. Strong brave centre halves, mad, crazy keepers and intelligent, cultured, inside rights.

The Park

The park was neutral ground and a chance for the middle-class kids to hide their school caps and blazers in the hedge and pretend they were working-class, which they seldom pulled off. These games were the jumpers for goalpost marathons that started when the park keeper opened the gates at 9.00 a.m. and finished when the gates were shut at dusk. Well, only until the park keeper had gone home for his kippers and brown bread. Then it was over the fence, a few torches in the trees and the magic truly began. The shafts of light contrasting with the dark shadows was probably the most exciting thing for a player to experience, even if they went on to win the World Cup.

The games would last all day with people coming and going depending on their teatimes, and the posh kids had to go back for lunch, choir practice and Sunday afternoon homework.

The game could start with three-a-side, building to twenty-a-side by mid-morning, before thinning out at around lunchtime. Then the early afternoon surge began with anything up to thirty-a-side.

There were three potential problems in the park. A grumpy park keeper, dog mess and picnic parties. Picnic parties on summer Sundays were a hazard. Rather than staying in the same spot, the picnic parties would spread out all over the park. There was nothing quite as bad as the sight of a tartan rug and a wicker basket to a street footballer.

There is nothing on earth that sounds the same as a Wembley Trophy ball coming down on top of a large pink blancmange. The sucking sound is reminiscent of a vet pulling his arm out of a constipated cow, and the splat that follows causes a wave of pink splodge to cover the pretty little velvet and lace clad, eight-year-old girls, whose screams even woke up the scrumpy drinkers on the park bench.

The Bowls Club

Every time a street footballer passed a bowls club, one look at the flat, bright green, billiard table-like surface would have them drooling. Why was such a brilliant footie pitch used exclusively by old people with plastic hips playing a game where you rolled a bit of wood along the floor?

The few kids that ever made it onto a bowling green talk of an out of body experience in which they are looking down at the ball which is rolling smoothly along the lush green carpet. Every pass was true and even, and every slide tackle gouged a deep trench any First World War soldier would have been proud of.

The consequences for the bowling fraternity were pretty serious as many lost the will to live as their sacred turf was hacked to pieces by the footie crazed youngsters.

Playground

What a laugh playground football was with all your school mates. The only thing that made school worthwhile and one of the few reasons kids would get up in the morning.

These days health & safety have stopped most playground football, but the local drug dealer outside the school gates is giving a new high to the kids that doesn't involve kicking around a bald tennis ball.

I attended a small grammar school of some 350 boys. Other than summer months, the only place to go at break times was the school playground. It was small with a five-foot wall surrounding it.

There was always a game of footie going on, so unless the likes of Appleby and Barrington-Babb wanted to be steamrollered by thirty footballers all massed together in a big scrum you had to scale the wall pretty sharpish.

Remember, the school had 350 children, so with thirty playing football that left some 320 dangling precariously from the walls.

The boffins at the school who were not street football-wise would often turn their back on the raging inferno below, working out some chess moves or showing off their collection of Peruvian first day covers.

You would have thought that with their incredible knowledge of physics and a deep understanding of the Pythagoras theorem they would have prepared themselves for the inevitable.

Once, Cliff Parker, the hardest shot in the fourth year, wiped out the entire school quiz team of Ackford, Eden, Jennings and Clements with a right-foot volley. The situation was exacerbated in that the quiz team were due to appear in the TV final of *Top of the Form* against the girls from Stella Maris Convent that very evening.

The Beach

Westward Ho! is a long way from the Copacabana Beach in Rio, Brazil and the football was certainly not as skilful but we would not have swapped it for the world. And while the girls in Rio wore only a couple of bootlaces for bikinis, the girls on Westward Ho! Beach were more likely to be wearing anoraks, balaclavas and mittens.

One of the great pleasures in life was marking out a pitch with one of those long handled red beach spades that frequently took off a child's big toe when digging a castle moat in haste. When the sand was wet but firm you could mark out a proper pitch with six-yard areas, penalty boxes, halfway line and semi-circle. Magic! Buckets and spades for goalposts and you were away.

There were a number of obstacles to a good game on the beach and one of the main problems was the wind. If you did not have very close control of the ball a gust could rob you of possession and if you scored a goal, between the bucket and spade goalposts, and the wind was behind you, the 'keeper had a fifty-yard sprint to retrieve the ball before trying to jog back with a g-force wind giving him a receding hairline look.

The other problem was sunny days during the summer holidays when the beach was packed and there was so little room to play. Even if you went early you were soon surrounded by frowning dads in vests and women in headscarves looking to claim a spot for the day. Any ball that went off the pitch was bound to knock a young child's ice cream from their hand or hit a snoozing dad, reclining on a deck chair, smack on the forehead. After a few of these incidents the holidaymakers would unite and feel confident enough to invade the pitch and chuck you off.

The other negative was when it was boiling hot and some of the dads who had not planned on taking a dip were persuaded by their other halves to take the plunge wearing just their pants. 'Go on Cyril, don't be silly, they look just like trunks, no one will notice.' Well, I have never seen a pair of Speedos turn transparent and sag at the crotch thanks to a couple of pints of sandy, salt water.

Some of those visions of Y-front clad middle-aged men jogging up the beach still haunt me to this day. It is at the other end of the spectrum to Ursula Andress in *Dr No*.

Bathing in your pants is a singularly British thing and sadly I succumbed on a hot August bank holiday last year with the wife scolding me for being pathetic and saying that it would be the only chance that year to sample the delights of a dip in the sea. I spent a torturous three-minute spell among a gathering of 'Portuguese Men of War' who had nothing to do with Eusebio and Benfica, but as the dictionary puts it:

(Physalia of phylum Coelenterata live in the sea, in colonies, and have a large air-filled bladder on top and numerous hanging tentacles).

On the out-of-breath, semi-jog back up the beach I thought for a moment one had swum up the leg of my M&S boxers. But after most of Croyde Bay had drained from my pants I realised that everything was as it should be. However on that asthmatic journey back to the relative comfort of a hand towel and a now toasted tuna and sweet corn sandwich, I caught the startled face of a young lad with a ball tucked under his arm. Forty years on and yet another traumatised young footballer who would no doubt repeat the same mistake forty years hence.

As the tide came in and the pitch became too small for a proper game we would all became goalies as we threw the ball into the giant breakers and then had to try and keep it from reaching the beach. We all leaped in different directions as the ball bobbled on the frothing mass of water before squirming under our bodies with the force of the water. These were memorable moments and we would all choose to be a different 'keeper, Banks,

Springett, Yashin and co., with the winner being the one who made the most saves.

The beach held both the best and worst football experiences for the young player.

My Garden

My parents moved to a new house in 1963 which was in a lovely setting, nestling on a steep valley hillside with a view of the River Torridge in north Devon. The slope in the garden would have even challenged Sherpa Tenzing's climbing skills and if George Best had lived in that idyllic but impracticable location, I am sure he would never have become a household name, for he had hundreds of kids to play football with on the housing estates of Belfast. I, on the other hand, had a retired dentist and his wife living on one side and a mad woman in her late eighties on the other. Every time my ball went into her garden, which was frequently as it was at the bottom of the slope, she would attack it with nine inches of Sheffield stainless steel in such a frenzy that even a certain American Motel owner by the name of Bates, would have been proud. These neighbours hardly made good material for a quick game of 'three and in' before teatime.

Then there was the Barnes Wallis effect. This was when the ball went down our steep driveway, whizzed out into the lane, rebounded off the wall opposite and began to bounce, bounce, bounce down the lane.

There was a tight corner at the bottom, and cars, cyclists and pedestrians when turning the corner could be met by this orange sphere hurtling towards them at speeds only Donald Campbell in Bluebird had yet reached. By the time I had got to the bottom of our driveway there was mayhem in the lane and my Wembley Trophy ball was already bobbing on top of the River Torridge, carried out to sea on the spring tide, no doubt to be punctured, somewhere downstream, by the sharp claws of our only local celebrity and Salmon guzzler, Tarka the Otter.

The Bedroom

Many brothers shared bedrooms and this was paradise for those who wanted to play twenty-four-hour football.

With single beds placed at each end of the room, players took it in turns to try and score by hitting the wall behind the opponent's bed.

With a springy mattress to dive on, the favourite game was Banks v Yashin. Lev Yashin was the Russian 'keeper who dressed like a referee, all in black. He became a bit of a cult figure in England during the sixties and vied for best 'keeper in the world with Banks.

The game varied from brothers to bedrooms, with extra points awarded for hitting the wall and then rebounding to hit the 'keeper on the head. Extra points were also awarded by some for goals scored by various pieces of bedroom furniture such as the wardrobe.

A light ball was normally used as a Wembley Trophy in such a confined space could cause extensive collateral damage.

A heavy ball hitting the overhead light was also both spectacular and a regular occurrence that led to many thick ears around the country.

There was talk of a boy up Rayleigh Hill who, while making a wonderful save, full-stretch, ended up two floors below in the cellar, still on the bed and still clutching the ball. What we used to refer to as 'a Lev Yashin moment'.

French Campsites

The family – my parents, older brother, younger sister and I went for our first camping trip to France in 1967. Flush with the World Cup win a year before, my brother and I felt like a second wave of missionaries going out into the world to show Johnny Foreigner how to play foot-ball the 'proper way'.

The old family Ford Zephyr was full to the gunnels with camping gear. My father must have bought the tent from Baden Powell's grandfather and I would hazard a guess that the last time it had been used would have been as part of a field hospital in the Crimean War. No doubt some of the survivors of the Charge of the Light Brigade were patched up under this piece of grim canvas.

The other thing that was responsible for the axle being three-inches from the road was hundreds of tins of food.

We were going to the greatest food nation on earth but my dear mother had packed under seats, in door pockets, glove box and wherever she could, tins of Fray Bentos steak and kidney pie, mince (which always contained bits of tube which I took to be lung) baked beans, Spam, corned beef, new potatoes that tasted like soap, Carnation Milk, peaches, pineapple chunks, Ambrosia cream rice, pork luncheon meat, processed peas, packets of Instant Whip, and, to impress the French, and my mother's only concession to fine dining, four tins of Marks & Spencer's chunky chicken in white wine sauce.

The other thing she took was a large thermos filled with butter. There must have been twelve blocks of Anchor, unwrapped and squeezed into the tartan container which had all melted by the time we reached Rennes.

I can just picture her now standing in the hallway at four in the morning in her blue and white-striped pedal pushers reading out the checklist: 'Passports, boat tickets, Dramamine, bathing costumes, towels and large thermos of butter'.

Did she really think that two adults and three children would consume nearly a block of butter a day? I can understand if we were making a bid for the South Pole but not the French Atlantic coast in August.

In defence of my mum, who was a great 'English' cook, this was in the days when olive oil could only be found in chemists and was used to pour in your ears when they were blocked with wax. No wonder the rest of Europe were not overly anxious to get us into the Common Market. The only thing we had to dress salads with then was Heinz salad cream.

The other rather eccentric holiday behaviour came from my father who was fantastic in a crisis.

You could come home from school one day and announce, 'Dad I have got something important to tell you. I have just murdered the Maths teacher and got all the girls in the street pregnant.'

'Don't worry son, put it down to experience.'

But put him behind the wheel of a car on a family holiday and he displayed some of the most bizarre human behaviour I have ever witnessed.

Just two hundred yards from leaving home he would start to sweat and begin shouting. 'The car is so heavy with all this camping gear that I am fighting with the wheel' (cue exaggerated steering wheel technique). Driving a simple family saloon on holiday was for him like going twenty-five rounds with Mick MacManus.

He also owned a battered brief case which he called, for reasons unknown, an attaché case. I presumed he must be carrying around the Treaty of Versailles but I guess it was probably because of the importance which he gave to the items inside, for when you came to a place where you would have to show some kind of documentation, such as at the ferry terminal, border crossing or camping site, he would scream, 'Camping Carnet – where's the attaché case?'

If it was not open and right by his side, with the Camping Carnet sticking out a few inches more than the rest of the documentation, he would go mental.

His whole holiday was based on how far the attaché case was from him. He used it as a pillow in the tent and even walked with it along the beach, wearing the most ridiculously tight, ball-hugging, shorts.

We hired a dinghy at one point and he had the attaché case firmly clenched between his legs as he rowed.

A year later and we were camping on

the French Riviera when he found out that the Russians had just walked into Czechoslovakia. He was all for packing up and heading home. I think he thought it was just a Russian ruse to drive across Western Europe, on through Germany and into France, cutting off the family Zephyr around Auxerre, capturing their intended target all along, dad's battered, British-made attaché case.

The idea was to drive through the Loire Valley area and onto our final destination at Penvins on the Atlantic coast.

As we motored down the tree-lined straight roads, my brother and I pored over the Michelin camping guide looking for sites that had the football pitch symbol. Many of the municipal sites run by the local councils either had a pitch or were next to one. The amenities on these sites were a bit more basic and might have had only cold showers, but as we explained to our mum: 'The goals may even have nets!'

The first site was in Argentat and the campsite was on the side of a lake.

We made our excuses by saying we would look for drinking water while mum and dad put up the big top.

What, in fact, we were doing was looking for GB stickers on cars and potential British players for a game against the Frogs.

While the most glorious cooking smells wafted over to our tent from the French, Italians and Spanish, we made do with a Spam salad.

Later we played football like a Spam salad while the French played liked a coq au vin and crepe suzette.

When we arrived at Penvins a few days later, we were on the wrong end of a six-game losing streak as the holiday went from bad to worse.

The site was heaving with GB stickers and by the second day we had managed to rustle up a team of eleven players. One had once had a trial at Scunthorpe, another played for Oxford Boys and we had a lad from Scotland who had played for East Fife Juniors.

We found a group of French boys playing near the beach and we challenged them to a game at noon the next day.

The British team went down to the venue, a stretch of sand between the dunes and the campsite. We practised our shooting and some of the players looked really good.

The French only had nine players so we already had the advantage. That advantage lasted all of twelve seconds before one of their midfield players ran through and scored. They had three outstanding players, who completely controlled the game, and by the end we were mere spectators as the trio took it in turns to score. Three of the players, I would say, were a year or so older than me. And when the last goal went in I made one last despairing dive and landed face down in the sand.

The frustration welled deep inside and I wept into the sand. I wept because we had just been outplayed by a bunch of Frogs, I wept because England were beaten by

Scotland in their first game at Wembley after the World Cup.

I wept because the Frogs were not all saying how brilliant we were in the war for driving the Germans out of their country, I wept because our pet rabbits Fizzy and Pop had been killed six months before by a Jack Russell–Border terrier cross and I wept because I would inevitably end up bald like my dad. Then I could cry no more and I was fine.

Seventeen years later and I am back in France on holiday with my wife and I go into a nearby bar to watch France play Spain in Euro 1984. Something about the way three of the French players moved and ran with the ball jolted some long ago memory bank and I nearly choked on my jambon baguette. Had I played against Platini, Tigana and Giresse all those years ago at Penvins?

Back to 1967 – it was a desolate walk back to the tent, but at least we were cheered up by mum's late lunch of tinned mince with bits of lung, soapy, tinned new potatoes and processed peas. A proper British meal.

We tried to find the French lads the next day and challenge them to a game of cricket. I wanted to see how the one they called Michel, who'd scored most of the goals, would cope with no pads on with a fast swinging googly, disguised as a leg break, from a proper cricket ball, but they were nowhere to be found.

The Vicarage Lawn

Heaven knows why I became a choirboy. I think my father thought it was a good idea and made my brother and I go. He was an agnostic and never went to church but I think he thought it was spiritually a good thing for us to do.

But I was not that spiritual, having to get up early every Sunday and cycle the six-mile round trip to St Mary's and back, wasting valuable footie time.

Then there was choir practice on a Friday night. In the darker evenings we would hide behind the gravestones and shine torches on our faces while jumping up and making ghoulish noises – great if it was Mrs Witts, the choir mistress, but bad news if it was Mr Perkins, the organist, who had long greasy hair and rode a motorbike.

He wore giant gauntlets and would chase you round the gravestones, cursing and cuffing you around the head.

On the brighter side you got one shilling and sixpence a year wages, which we threatened to go on strike over each year, but we got half a crown for every wedding which was 'top dollar' back then.

The only problem came when the older boys decided they would run a sweep on who would cry first at the wedding. The older boys got first pick and the golden rule was, the bigger the hat, the bigger the tears.

The younger lads got fed up with losing their hard-earned wages so at one wedding we drew straws as to who would punch who in the first minutes of the service and split the winnings among us and stop the older boys' monopoly. I had to wallop Galliford and did so with such gusto that he bawled for the entire service and had to be led out.

The betting stopped from then on and we were able to spend our dosh on comics and sweets at Jones the newsagents next to the church.

The real benefits of being in the choir happened twice a year at church functions at the vicarage when we were allowed to play football on the lawn.

The lawn was pristine and nearly as good as the bowls club green. Jackets and jumpers were laid down as goalposts and we played for several hours. Such was the intensity of the games and the sheer joy of playing on such a wonderful surface that we even missed the England v Argentina World Cup quarter-final at Wembley on television.

Those games on the vicarage lawn have stayed with me for more than forty years.

The games were not everyone's cup of

tea as the vicar's wife had green fingers and each year her garden was in danger of being ruined by the football thirsty choirboys.

The vicar knew how much we appreciated his gesture every year, although I think it came at a price for him as she was always scowling at us from the front pew in the church.

THE GAMES WE PLAYED

*Play is the universal language
of children*
Anon

It didn't matter where you were in the world, Dakar or Didcot, Milan or Maidstone, Sao Paulo or Salcombe, Buenos Aires or Bognor Regis, you all did the same – played games. That is what children do and they are the experts, not some fifty-year-old fat bloke in a tracksuit.

There was no warm-up or laps, dynamic stretches or drills, and if there were enough of you, you played a game.

If you were on your own, or with just a couple of your mates, you kicked a ball against a wall.

Spot/'Wallie'/Football Squash

You usually played this with two or three people. The first player kicked the ball against the wall and then it was the next person's turn to kick it before the ball stopped. You were also only allowed one touch. This continued until someone missed by either kicking the ball over the wall, usually to the accompaniment of breaking glass or the ball either did not reach the wall or stopped before you could get to it.

Each player had three lives and it was a knock-out competition with the last person remaining the winner.

This game was brilliant in improving your shooting, touch and anticipation. The clever ones could judge by the angle the previous player kicked the ball and at what speed, where the ball would land and get into position early.

Three-and-in

This game is as old as the Egyptian Pyramids and as British as bread and dripping and ingrowing toe nails.

It was usually played with just a few players scoring into one goal. When the goalkeeper had let in three goals you swapped 'keepers. The other players set each other up and it had to be a spectacular goal to count. Some kids just didn't get it and would blast the ball from a mere six inches from the line and celebrate like an idiot.

Those in the know would always give the 'keeper hope and the perfect goal was in the top corner from a fair distance away, but not hit too hard so that the 'keeper still had a thirty per cent chance to get a finger-tip to it. This also meant the ball would not go too far a distance to be retrieved.

If you blasted the ball and you had no nets, the beaten 'keeper, hands on hips, would extract some revenge by looking at where the ball had landed, some 100 yards away, and then look at you and spit out: 'You can get that!'

You always had to give him hope so that he would not trudge off disconsolate with his ball. This was an incredible skill to master – technique, psychology, and diplomacy, all in one volley.

If it was a great goal you would spend half an hour doing action replays of the whole move and going back to the start when you were not satisfied with the realism of your wonder goal.

It was a real art to both shoot and dive in slow motion, more of an art in fact than playing the proper game.

The game was even better when played in the dark with torches in the trees, or in the mud for diving or in the snow and risking the chapped legs of this book's title.

It was also very important to commentate on the game in the third person as you played. You would each be a different player. The most common phrase used in the latter part of the sixties in most streets, playgrounds and parks was 'Bagsie be Bestie'.

The commentary would last as long as you had the ball so it would go something like this.

Player One: 'Best, jinks round one player, jinks round another and pulls the ball back.'

Player Two: 'To Greaves who cleverly controls the ball and lays it off for Peters.'

Player Three: 'Who shoots and...'

Player Four: 'Oh great save by Yashin!'

Goal celebrations were important but there was nothing like the variety there is today with somersaults, rocking babies, shirts off and Elvis impressions with the corner flag.

You could choose from just three celebrations.

The Matthews/Finney, no nonsense handshake, pats on the back and now let's get on with the game celebration.

The Denis Law celebration where you run with your arm aloft, or the Bobby Charlton, Helmut Haller celebration, run five yards, jump and punch the air, run five yards, jump and punch the air, until you are back in your position.

Headers & Volleys

Basically the same as three-and-in only you

could only score with a header or a volley. There was always a fierce debate about whether a half-volley was classed as a volley and many a game was finished early with the ball owner going home in a huff.

For some unknown reason in north Devon we called this game Gerries, and no one seemed to know why?

I presume it was short for Germans, as that was what we called them in the endless games of war we played with our own home-made machine gun noises that sounded like someone laughing with a stutter.

The boys' comics we read were full of war stories and how the heroic exploits of brave British servicemen were defeating the cowardly Gerries on land, sea and air. Most comic strips appeared to have the immortal line as a British Commando shot yet another German,

'Take that Fritz, you square-headed sausage eater!'

Luckily my politics were more influenced by the *Beano* than *Hotspur*.

Wembley/World Cup

Depending on which generation you belonged to, this game was very popular and has spread to many other English speaking countries, but talk to anyone from Europe about the game and they give you a blank stare. Earlier generations knew this game as Wembley, but my son's generation, indeed it is still very popular today, know it as World Cup.

It is another game played with one goal and a neutral goalkeeper. All the players are divided into teams, singles or doubles. Every individual or pair is against each other and it is done as a knock-out.

Rules change, but my son plays it in a version where there may be as many as eight pairs. The first round is played and when you score a goal you go through to the next round.

This goes down to the last two pairs, and when one scores, the other is knocked out, so seven pairs go into the next round and so on.

My son and his friends were obsessed with World Cup and these games went on from one break time to another and then continued after school.

Kerby

The game is also known as Kerbys in some parts. Two players stand opposite each other on the street. The first player chips the ball and tries to hit the opposite kerb. If it hits the kerb and rolls back to your side of the road you get a point and another go. If it hits the kerb and bounces back up without hitting the road and you catch the ball it is worth three points. Anything else and it is your opponent's turn.

The Dutch Brick Game

They played very different games on the continent and a Dutch friend of mine living in the southern region of the Netherlands played a game where each player brought along a brick.

They would put the brick down and have to defend it while trying to knock down their opponents' brick with the ball.

They played a similar game which was based on the street where they lived. The back of each house came out on to a lane and each of the houses had a gate. Each player defended his own gate (home) while trying to score in one of the other player's gates.

Other people's experiences

(On A Street Where You Live)

ZINEDINE ZIDANE

Zidane learnt his sublime skills playing with his friends on the gravel of Place de la Tartane, the central square in La Castellane, a tough council estate in the northern suburbs of Marseille. The area was known in French as a 'quartier difficile'. The area was made up of first and second generation immigrants from North Africa.

Everything I have achieved in football is due to playing in the streets with my friends.

PETER HUSSEY
Football Development Officer, Southwick village, Near Trowbridge Wiltshire.

When I was younger (9-16) I lived in a cul-de- sac and we regularly set up a mini-pitch with a deck chair at each end as the goals (small target between the legs of the chair) and played with a tennis ball or anything that resembled one, as long as it was round, and we used the kerbs for wall passes.

Just after Christmas we used to go all out and use unwanted talcum powder and mark out lines.

And when wheelie bins made an introduction to this country we were given an amazing portable goal on wheels. As you can imagine the shout of 'car coming', echoed round the estate as we rapidly moved the goals for the passing car to drive through.

Also on our local playing field

we and many others used the wall of a maintenance shed for many games, which was great, especially if you had done the rounds calling on everyone, and no one was available. You could still go out on your own and practise your shooting or have target practice without having to run miles to collect the ball. Also as a 'keeper, practising your reactions against the wall was great.

Nothing used to stop us playing and the highlight of the week was half-time on a Sunday morning, when we could, for a brief moment play in full goals with nets.

Fifteen minutes of dreams, oh the memories.

BOBBY CHARLTON

Bobby was born and raised, with brother Jack, in Ashington, a mining village in Northumberland. The boys played in the local streets and park.

> *I always found the game easy and never had any difficulty controlling the ball, passing it or running with it. When I was growing up I used to play in our local park for about ten hours a day. All the older lads wanted me on their side, so I must have been a decent player.*

DAVE RAMZAN

Grassroots football coach, Greenwich, London.

> *Although never playing football to a very high standard, we did play football back in the late sixties in some very odd*

places. In the holds of empty Thames river barges, under a motorway on a huge enclosed ramp holding up the road (it was very dark) and on bomb sites that were still plentiful during the fifties and sixties.

On many occasion we went down with twisted and skinned ankles after tripping over a brick sticking up out of the playing surface.

Street football was played on a cobbled street down by the River Thames, where the goal areas were the kerbs on each side of the street, and goals were marked out in chalk on the brick walls behind. On many occasions we would play on grass in Greenwich Park until dark, having to climb over the high fence after closing, then being chased off by the 'Parkie'.

Apart from occasionally at school, we never played on marked out pitches unless playing an actual match. It never did Paul Elliott or Rio Ferdinand any harm as both went to the same school as me and other football mad friends.

STANLEY MATTHEWS

Stan lived on Seymour Street in the Hanley area of Stoke on Trent. His early football was played near his house.

I'd make for a piece of waste ground opposite our house where the boys from the neighbourhood gathered for a kick about. Coats would be piled for posts and the game of football would get under way. In fine weather it would be as many as twenty-a-side, in bad weather a hardened dozen or so made six-a-side.

In Stan's day the kids refereed their own games.

> *We didn't need a referee; we accepted the rules of the game and stuck by them. For us not to have done so would have spoilt the game for everyone. It taught us that you can't go about doing what you want because there are others to think of and if you don't stick to the rules, you spoil it for everyone else. Of course, that was not a conscious thought at the time, but looking back those kick about games on the waste ground did prepare us for life.*

DAVID ROCHE

Grassroots football coach, Bitton, Rugby, Warwickshire.
> *We played on the fields at the*

back of our houses, jumpers for goalposts. The age range was from seven to fifteen during the week nights and up to fifteen-a-side. It was not unusual for scores to be 45-38. Then for a bit of spice, our road would play the other roads at the school pitch; typical English get stuck in affair. 'Our street is better than yours'.

On Sundays the dads and granddads (mainly Scots) would appear for an all out Braveheart affair. Kids kicking lumps out of the adults and learning from the school of hard knocks.

Oh yes, and your dribbling was developed by going around the cow pats or through them, as it was a more direct route, while at the same time increasing our

> *spatial awareness by avoiding the brook that ran alongside the field.*
> *They were great days, a real community spirit and real fun.*

TOM FINNEY

Tom played in the fields and streets around Holme Slack in Preston pretending he was the next Alex James, his hero.

> *The kickabouts we had in the fields and on the streets were daily events, sometimes involving dozens of kids. There was so many bodies around you had to be flippin' good to get a kick. Once you got hold of the ball, you didn't let it go too easily. That's where I first learned about close control and dribbling.*
> *It was a world of make-believe – were children more imaginative in those days?*

– and although we only had tin cans and school caps for goalposts, it mattered not a jot. In my mind, this basic field was Deepdale and I was the inside-left, Alex James. I tried to look like him, run like him, juggle the ball and body swerve like him. By being James, I became more confident in my own game. He never knew it, but Alex James played a major part in my development.

DAVID COCKINGS

Grassroots football coach, Irchester, Northants (Also birthplace of Phil Neal, Liverpool & England).

The close where we lived was our training ground. In those days (mid '70s) families only had one car, which the husbands used to go to work in, so during the day the street was deserted.

We then progressed to the field at the end of the road (Station Road). It's never been used for agriculture and only rarely for grazing, but you never see kids playing there now. And finally we thought we had really made it when the council built a playing field on the edge of the village (the edge of the Arkwright Estate, off Austin Close) and stuck up two goalposts.

Away games were played on the old bowling green; it was flatter than the village team's pitch despite being disused for twenty years.

ANDY BROWN

Grassroots football coach, Hackney, East London.

We had a number of 'stadiums' within a five-minute walk of our house and with quite a few housing estates around; there was always someone to play football with.

In two of the estates there were hard courts, surrounded with big high fences. There was also the park (Hackney Downs) which had a grass pitch and a new Astroturf pitch with floodlights. This turned out to be one of the hardest surfaces to play on because as well as having to deal with the broken glass from the floodlights and dead animals, some kids had made vain attempts to set light to it. One was nearly successful and had left a four-foot wide patch on one of the wings that you had to avoid at all costs.

But the best 'stadium' of all for me was the tunnel that ran under the railway track to the park. It was curved and I would spend hours kicking a ball through it trying to get it to roll round the tunnel – like the minis in the Italian Job. Never did manage it!'

NOBBY STILES

Nobby grew up in Manchester.

I went to the old burial ground in Collyhurst where as a six or seven-year-old I played football with my mates on the upturned gravestones. It was a little difficult to find. There were some barred gates and I had to find my way through some workshops that I didn't easily recall. Hedges and bushes were overgrown.
But then magically, it was

there – the old place with the gravestones dating back to the eighteenth century, stretching out and providing the pitch for the ghosts of my past; and the ghosts came alive again, racing for the ball, shoving you into the wet grass and the shale, and crying 'twat' and other endearments when you nicked it away from them and kept your feet on the greasy stones and dribbled over the memorial lines to some long-gone beloved husband or wife or, tragically common, some darling infant.

We never thought we were violating anyone's memory. We were just enjoying being young.

DAVID WILLIAMS

Grassroots football coach, London Colney, Hertfordshire.

I lived in Summerfield Close, a cul-de-sac, and there was a nice field outside, so we were lucky, unless the ball went in to number one house, as they were evil. The two brothers had both been inside for GBH. They used to play with us until one of our mates called his mum a name, and we were all laughing. From then on if they were in no-one would want to get the ball, for fear of being beaten up, although now I don't think they would have done it.

We also had driveways built in the seventies with two garages between houses.

Each garage had a metal door. We would have our garage door up, that was the goal. Every time you missed you would hear BANG, causing much annoyance to all the

*neighbours. My dad gave me
a smack after he had told me
many times to stop kicking the
ball against the garage door.*

*We once played on a lake
that had frozen over (Colney
Lakes) that was fantastic fun.
We came back to play the
following day, to see someone
had made a hole in the ice.
It was scary when you were
sliding towards the hole,
lucky no one fell in. It was a
great way to pass a few hours,
before the ice started to thaw.*

GEORGE BEST

George Best played for hours on a patch
of grass some one hundred yards from his
front door on the Cregagh Estate.

*Literally as soon as I could walk,
I had a ball at my feet. One of
the first photographs taken
of me was outside my granny*

*and granddad Withers' house
when I was about 13 months
old, with a ball at my feet. It
didn't matter what sort of ball
it was – plastic, a tennis ball,
anything I could kick around.
Sometimes I would even take
a ball to bed with me.*

KRIS BELLHORN

Grassroots football coach, Walnutport,
Pennsylvania, USA.

*My neighbour had a side lot
next to the house (corner
of Third Ave and Williams
Ave) just big enough to play
football. We used soda cans
for goals, and clothing for
touchlines ... shirts and socks
usually ... the occasional boot
if we needed ... then we all
played barefoot to make it
fair!*

JUAN ROMAN RIQUELME

The great Argentinean playmaker learned his trade playing with his friends in the capital city Buenos Aires.

> Where I come from, Don Torcuato (a neighbourhood in the outskirts of Buenos Aires) we are lucky to have a lot of open spaces and fields. I spent my whole childhood playing football with my friends, from dawn to dusk, always in open spaces. Sometimes we'd stop for a bite to eat and then carry on. I still live there – when I go to Buenos Aires – and I still play football there with those same friends.

RICHARD WEBB

Grassroots football coach, North London, England.

> We used to play footie in loads

of places in North London as kids.

First, there was outside in the street when the only cars we had to dodge was a claret and blue Ford Poplar owned by the bloke next door, a gold Mk II Jag owned by the right old 'Luvvie' actor type from about five doors away (he also owned a miniature poodle with ribbons!) and last but not least, the bright yellow GPO van (can't remember the make or owner). It would be coats for goalposts on either side of the road and when we got bored, we added the condition that you could only score from a headed ball that had first rebounded up in the air off of the kerb.

In between us and next door was an eight-yard gap with a huge metal up and over shutter which led into an old coach station. When there were just two of us we would use the concrete sides of the steps to the houses either side of the gap as goals. When we wanted to hone our goalkeeping skills we would use the big metal shutter as the goal. If you let one in the noise was like the gong at the start of the J Arthur Rank films which would then incur the wrath of the neighbourhood. So you had to be as good as Gordon Banks or you got a clip round the ear hole from one of the neighbours who was on nights! (The men seemed to be built like brick shithouses back then and had hands like dustbin lids!)

Then there was what we called 'round the back'. A concrete playground behind where *we lived which was split into two. One side was swings, a roundabout, giggling girls and the park keeper's hut. The other was an expanse of concrete surrounded by chain-link fencing fixed to concrete posts. If you played with other kids your age then a goal was the width of one gap between these posts. If you played with older kids twice your age (I suppose they were teenagers but they seemed much older) a goal was the width of two of these gaps. Matches could be anything from one v one up to about twenty-five v twenty-five I suppose.*

The older ones always helped the little kids by laying goals on for them and giving them loads of encouragement. Each time you played you played to either improve, or impress the girls. It depended on your age. When the park keeper had locked up and gone home, we would all climb back over and pick up where we left off. The street lighting took care of that!

Then there was the cinder pitch in Rosemary Gardens, complete with goals, fence and first aid station! Boy, was that needed at times! It was like playing on a huge slippery, moving, cheese grater. If you didn't learn to defend by staying on your feet like Bobby Moore, then the first aid station is where you ended up … needing a full skin graft down one side of your body! I could go on and on.

BOBBY MOORE

The captain of England's World Cup win- ning team did not have it all his own way down at the local park. A big learning curve for the great man.

> *On Sunday mornings at about ten o'clock, maybe twenty to twenty-five young lads would meet in Barking Park and invariably he was the last to be picked.*
>
> *Now imagine if we could have seen into the future and there is the future England captain and he is the last to be picked.*
>
> **Peter Buckle (Bobby's cousin)**

ANDY CHESTER

Grassroots football coach, Lutterworth, Leicestershire against the old Vedonis Factory Gates.

> *We used to play at the end of the street against the factory gates. Countless days spent climbing said gates to retrieve*

the ball after rather ambitious shots. This was everyone in the street, all ages, girls and boys and the next street too. We used to make a goal out of coats at the other end and all stand on the path if a car came.

DAVID GINOLA

Although David grew up in the beautiful South of France he was not distracted from his love of the beautiful game.

I was passionate about football from an early age. From the age of about two years old, as soon as I could walk, I was kicking a ball about. I have vivid memories of loving football from the moment I figured out how this plastic round thing could move – I think I was born to play football. It was my father who introduced me to the game when one day he just kicked me a football. We played together and he asked me what I thought. I replied: 'Yes, I like it,' and from then on I was never without a football tucked under my arm, always in the garden practising my skills.

I played football every evening in the street outside my house with all my friends. In the summer we would kick the ball around for hours, until the sky darkened at about 10.30pm. The game was interrupted only if a car came by and we all rushed to the side of the road until it passed. Sometimes we played against a nearby wall, marking out goals and inventing rules.

Randall Northam

Publisher, Plymouth

At my grammar school in the 1950s (and presumably for some time after) each class had a 'form ball' which was an old case ball which had to be collected from the sports master at the start of the lunch hour and then returned. On our third day this group of eleven-year-old first years found they had no form ball. The problem was that our form teacher, obviously not knowing our characters in those early days, had appointed a very weedy boy called Marshall to collect the ball. He, having no interest in football, had forgotten or couldn't be bothered. The only thing that stopped us battering him to a pulp was that he was the headmaster's son's best friend.

Thereafter the ball was always collected by one of about five of us who were certain never to forget and if they did could be easily beaten up.

Then there was the time I wanted a Subbuteo set for Christmas (aged ten) and my parents decided what I really wanted was a football game played on a raised pitch with the players controlled underneath by magnets. The pitch was shiny and slippery and the players impossible to control. My dad persuaded me on Boxing Day to have a game with him and I threw the bloody thing on the floor after five minutes.

DAVE GODLEY

Academy Coach who played in Holland and Brazil.

> *The most incredible thing we saw was in Brazil when walking through this huge square in the city centre with a beautiful cathedral. There was a bunch of kids playing the most skilful football with an empty coke bottle.*
>
> *They used a tree at one end and a jumper at the other as goals and played the most intense football with players falling on the hard ground, scraping knees, getting cuts and grazes. One player stood out, flicking this coke bottle up and volleying it against the tree for a goal.*
>
> *Back home in Lacock Wiltshire, I loved shooting and was lucky that my next door neighbour,*

who was a couple of years younger than me, liked playing in goal. We played against the shed door and I would shoot, volley and take penalties. I must have scored thousands of goals this way which was great for a striker.

TOM WATT

Writer, broadcaster, actor, North London.
I grew up in a residential street in Holloway in the 1960s. The way the street was laid out it was mainly terraced houses, but I lived on the other side of the street next to a builder's yard which had these big, black-painted doors.
At the other end of the street was a dairy depot with a big wall running alongside it. So we played at either one or other end of the street.

I played from about aged seven or eight but didn't really get into football properly until the World Cup in '66.

You could just about have a small-sided game at the end of the street as there were walls on both sides.

If there was no-one around, I would kick the ball against the builders' yard doors, much to the annoyance of the neighbours. If there were a few of us we would always play a game called Brazilia.

You can play this with a 'keeper or not. One person crosses and everyone else competes to score. You could only score with headers or volleys. If the ball hit the ground it had to go back to the person doing the crossing. We did that almost every day for four or five years. The game was entirely designed to do the best bits in football, headers and volleys!

I was playing at the primary school just up the road as well. There was a bottom playground which had goals painted on the walls. There were some quite good players and Terry Burton who was a couple of years older than me went on to play professionally.

There was a game every lunch break and, because I loved the game, I would join in with the older boys. Often as not they would make me go in goal, but that was fine as I was involved. It was more of a social thing, a free for all with fifteen or twenty-a-side.

Later I got friendly with some kids on an estate about half a mile away. It was an estate that was built around a patch *of green and we would have scratch games.*

That kind of football carried on through secondary school.

I was never really involved with organised football but I remember even at university – I was at Manchester – on our way back to London we would spot a likely field in Derbyshire and just stop the car and go and play football for an hour or so. By then Brazilia had been refined and you had to score with a diving header.

THE ENEMIES OF STREET FOOTBALL

We used to play in the streets, coats down as goals, 5-a-side. They were happy days those, great days. You never thought of anything else but playing football, in the back streets on the cobbles, until the Bobby came and shifted you.
Tom Finney

Policemen

Have always been anti street footballers and think you are just up to mischief rather than honing your talents to win England another World Cup.

Were they never kids?

The council

Whoever thought of putting up signs saying 'No Ball Games'? What a complete waste of taxpayers' money.

Someone had to come up with the idea of how to stop children having fun, then design and make the signs before driving round and putting them up in all the best footie hot spots.

So you can't play in the street or near houses, so you go down the park to find that the same killjoy has put up a 'keep off the grass' sign.

What part are they playing in the grand scheme of things?

Goal hangers

Things I would rather happen to me or be called, other than goal hanger.

Any swear word; including the one questioning your parentage and the one implying that your mother had an extra occupation other than working in the classified ads department at the *Leatherhead Gazette*.

Receive the black spot from Blind Pugh.

Snog Deborah Smyth from form 2B.

Walk around naked for a week with my underpants on my head while reciting 16th century Flemish poetry.

Support Chelsea (well, maybe that is going too far for a Fulham fan).

Be transported back to plague-ravaged London as a boil-lancer.

Eat nothing but lemon curd for a month.

Goal hangers are a breed. Often a loner or only child who does the equivalent of goal hanging in everything they do. They would always be found hanging around the park alone, looking for a game. The scary thing is they are completely oblivious to what they are doing and why everyone loathes them. If when they scored they just slotted the ball home it would not be so bad, but they usually toe-punt the ball as hard as they can, so that it goes for miles. This would be followed by the inevitable argument about who should go and get the ball.

When enough was enough both teams would agree to some new rules that would make things decidedly uncomfortable for the goal hanger, such as: 'The next goal must be scored from outside the line of that tree over there,' (about twenty yards from goal. It has to be a left foot volley (goal hangers are always right footed – a well known fact in street soccer circles) into the top corner of the goal.

The goal hanger could not execute such a shot and after a couple of feeble attempts would go and bother the ducks in the pond.

Big dogs

Little dogs were fine; especially Jack Russells who love dribbling the ball and whose jaws were not big enough to allow their gnashers to sink into it.

They could head a ball as well and were the Peles of the dog world.

The dogs I mean are those big dogs that posh people have, like Red Setters, Labradors and Golden Retrievers. All owned by people who love rugby and hate football.

The usual scenario is for you to look up in a match only to see one of these hounds bearing down on your prize possession, a brand new Wembley Trophy.

'Lady, heel, heel,' shouts the owner, who is still strolling lazily and making no attempt to physically restrain Beelzebub's pet pooch.

The inevitable happens and you hear the hiss of the ball being punctured. The owner eventually gets to the massacre site, but rather than apologising and handing over a pound for a new ball, they insist that Lady must drop the ball on command. 'Drop, drop' they repeat ninety-five times, before the spittle-covered blob of now useless plastic is let go.

'Oh good girl,' the owner chirps, patting her and fussing over her hysterically before giving her a Good Boy Choc drop for her endeavours, and walking off to the next bit of ball butchery, and another game ruined, further into the park.

Groundsman

Every other week we went down to watch Bideford FC play at the sports ground.

We always took a ball and as soon as the referee blew for half-time, *Penny Lane* by the Beatles would come wafting out of the PA system and we would run out onto the pitch and into one of the goals for a kick about.

Now I was a big Beatles fan but *Penny Lane* was the only song they had and they played it every game for three years. Considering the flip side to *Penny Lane* was *Strawberry Fields Forever* you would have thought the announcer could have aired that a few times instead.

Three minutes and forty-five seconds was the longest we ever managed to stay on the pitch before the loudest voice on the planet would scream 'Get off my pitch!'

He must have had special voice training to get it to travel so loudly and so far. No doubt he was the twin brother of the guy at the council and had been put on this earth to stop me having fun.

I am sure that most groundsmen would prefer that no games were played at all on their hallowed turf.

Professional room tidier

Or rather the lack of one.

The stock reply from your mum after letting her know you were going out to play was, 'You're going nowhere until you have tidied your room.'

The knee-jerk response of 'But I like my room untidy' was never clever and made sure your mum would check whether you had tidied up.

They were cunning those adults and should never have been under-estimated.

Little sisters

I love my sister dearly, but there was a time when I was less enamoured of her.

My brother and I were having a game of three-and-in against the sofa in the lounge one wet Sunday afternoon. With all the vases, ornaments and family heirlooms, the inevitable happened. A stray shot knocked mum's prize clock off the mantelpiece. All of this was witnessed by our little sister for her to store this useful ammunition for another time.

We managed to keep the charade of a working clock going for about a week by manually moving the hands every time the room was empty.

One day, when teasing my sister, I went a step too far and she spilled the beans. From then on she was known as Supergrass, and our revenge was swift and rather nasty as our sister still reminds us around the Christmas dinner table some forty years later.

Our mother bought her a bright red

winter coat which had a strange texture like foam. 'Foam coat, foam coat … nerks' we chanted.

Mum was really angry as our sister refused to wear the coat after a while and it was expensive.

The main revenge though was through music and my sister used to hide behind the sofa when The Crazy World of Arthur Brown performed the hit *Fire* on *Top of The Pops*.

She was also scared of a 45 record of loud, aggressive, Flamenco music my parents brought from Spain a couple of years previously.

These European singles had a large hole in the middle, and back then you could not buy an adaptor to fit the hole so you could never put the record dead in the centre of the turntable. Which meant the most peculiar screeching sound with jumps and clicks would howl out of the speakers.

A scheme was hatched and my brother brought his portable Dansette into the lounge and put his newly acquired copy of *Fire* on his player while I placed the Spanish 45 on my parent's gramophone.

We lured our little sister into the lounge and said we had a lovely story record of Winnie the Pooh to play her.

She sat down comfortably on a couple of cushions and began to suck her thumb contentedly. Simultaneously we put the records on and made for the door closing it with a bang and holding on to the doorknob to keep our prisoner captive.

At full volume the Dansette roared out,
I am the god of hell fire and I bring you
FIRE, I'll take you to burn.
FIRE, I'll take you to learn.

While on the gramophone, the Spanish dirge belted out and got stuck on a hideous shriek from the Spanish singer and a strange ghostly clicking from the castanets.

Our sister screamed and began to frantically pull at the door-handle, but we were on the other side, revelling in our wrong doing.

Head Teachers

Many teachers were brilliant and did everything they could to support the kids playing football, but some just did not get it. While writing this book my daughter told me of her and my son's experiences when they nearly brought the whole school to a standstill.

Baden's school, situated in a pretty Cotswold market town, had the reputation of being the best primary school in the district. There was never any controversy and one morning in 1996 seemed like any other as Daisy, year six, and Charlie, year three, walked to school.

The school had been a good place to play football at break-times with foam balls allowed in the playground and access to the school playing field in the summer term when the weather allowed.

The first shock of the day was at morning assembly when the headmistress announced that football in the playground had been banned.

There was no explanation why a game that must have been a school institution for generations was treated in this way and the whole school gasped in astonishment as many games were played by different classes and scraps of paper were passed around secretively in class with proposed teams for the lunchtime game.

When the bell rang for morning break, all the children trooped out and the ban was a hot topic. The consensus was that something should be done at lunchtime to register some kind of protest.

It started at noon, in a small way with Dan, Chris, Jamie and Daisy circling around the dinner ladies singing 'We want football, we want football.'

A few other members of year six joined the small but determined band and by 12.10 the numbers had grown to twenty-plus with the chant growing louder. The main four protagonists tied their blue school sweatshirts around their heads Rambo style while others further back swung their sweatshirts above their heads like South American football fans.

The number of children grew with year five joining. Charlie's best friend's brother composed another ditty to the *Teletubbies* theme tune and the two different chants began to interweave and become a battle cry for the children in the school.

At 12.20 the snaking column had grown to more than fifty children and had a menacing edge as children became more confident.

It was part Watt Tyler and the peasants' revolt and part Lord of the Flies.

Charlie and his year three friends had now tagged onto the end and the dinner ladies were out from lunch and trying to restore order.

At 12.30 the baying rabble of some 70 children screamed 'WE WANT FOOTBALL, WE WANT FOOTBALL.'

This was as big as the column would get as the headmistress, flanked by three teachers, rang the school bell while the dinner ladies blew on their whistles until they turned red.

A snatch squad of teachers and dinner ladies raided the front of the column and frog-marched the ring-leaders, still wearing their sweatshirts wrapped around their heads, to the assembly hall.

The column scattered and the younger ones managed to squirm free and hide in various places around the school playground.

Many however were not so lucky and within five minutes some forty children were sitting cross-legged on the assembly hall floor.

The teachers were apoplectic with rage and very startled as nothing like this had happened before at the school.

The children who were caught were given detention and not allowed to talk. The headmistress gave them all a stern telling off and the issue was brought up yet again with the ring-leaders named and shamed at the next morning's assembly.

To this day football has not been re-instated although a couple of years later year six were allowed to play one lunch-time a week in the winter on the school field.

For a brief moment the kids were in charge and fighting for what they saw as their game and the injustice of the school's decision.

Eleven years later and more than thirty per cent of schools have so far banned football in the playground.

With obesity and mental health major headline news due to the lack of outdoor play for children, it makes no sense to take away their game

REDSTAR UNITED AND THE EUROPEAN ADVENTURE

We played until our legs gave way – scores of 15-13 were not uncommon – and I never stopped running. I tried to make up in enthusiasm what I lacked in physical presence for all the boys were much bigger than I was, or so it felt.

Football united the kids. You didn't have to call for your mates; simply walking down the street bouncing a ball had the Pied Piper effect. We could all smell a game from 200 yards.

Tom Finney

In 1966, England's World Cup winning year, and with my garden football capers at an all-time low, after having my ball confiscated for teasing my little sister by saying 'Nerks Snodgrass' after everything she said, I literally got on my bike and looked for a team to play for.

A school friend, Andrew Cordell, and his younger brother Jonathan, who we always called Socks, had a patch of grass next door to their home and had asked me to come for a kick about. The grass was so tall that we had to borrow hedge-cutters and spend a whole weekend cutting down the pampas, expecting to find poisonous snakes, treasure, a lost civilisation, the Mary Celeste in dry dock and a Japanese soldier waiting for orders from his Emperor. What we found, in fact, was a rusty watering can and a dead rat.

We made our own goalposts and painted them with the wrong paint, which ten years later had still not dried.

By the side of the pitch there was a rusting Hillman Minx, with no wheels, which we made the home dressing-room, and a plastic wigwam covered in mould which we called the away dressing-room.

I don't remember anyone ever using the away dressing-room, as Andrew said he thought badgers did their business in there and that they could also take your face off with their sharp claws if you disturbed them.

These tales left no real incentive to explore the interior of Mini-Haha's love nest.

We were so lucky to have our own little ground but it was next to the main Bideford to Westward Ho! road, which in the summer became thick with traffic.

It was always when we were playing with our trusty Wembley Trophy ball that someone would clear it into row Z of our imaginary grandstand and onto the B3235 and straight under the number two bus or lorry.

The noise that came from the ball bursting was horrendous and we would have a little burial ceremony by the side of the pitch.

These were the start of some really good times, but you can only get so much mileage continually playing two against one.

We decided to start our own team and call it Redstar United, as it sounded vaguely skilful and foreign.

We loved the big games down the park to which we cycled every week. Although brilliant fun, these were controlled by much larger boys in their teens and even though we were still only nine, we had bigger plans – to play in Europe.

The football bible at the time was *Charles Buchan's Football Monthly,* and I was besotted with the magazine.

I read it from cover to cover religiously every month, but the two things that I re-read a thousand times over were the adverts for football jerseys and the classified adverts in the back, especially the section, 'foreign teams wanted to play'.

The three of us saved up our pocket money until we had enough to put an advert in the magazine:

'Redstar United, a junior team from north Devon, want to play teams from abroad.'

I was first up every morning, eagerly waiting for the postman, and after a week of gut-wrenching disappointment an envelope with 'REDSTAR UNITED FC' in big capital letters fell onto the door mat.

I don't think I have ever been as excited as at that very moment. That includes the World Cup win and my first ever kiss with Ann Mole at a village barn dance some seven years later. The fact that she kissed me while I was wearing a pink shirt with white shields, heavily stained by Branston pickle after an accident with my barn dance ploughmans', and a pair of purple, flared, cords was an achievement in itself.

We presumed the team must be in the European Cup as the letter was on proper headed notepaper, although the name, Elizabeth United from Guernsey did not ring any immediate bells. Redstar United were in Europe.

We needed funds and players quickly or we thought we might experience the wrath of FIFA for pulling out of a European fixture. The main thing we were worried about was getting a Redstar pennant to exchange at kick-off on our Euro jaunt.

Andrew's mother had been given a box of plain chocolate liqueurs from a distant aunt at Christmas and we would raffle these by going from door to door.

We figured we could get enough money for a team to travel out, plus kit and pennant.

After a week we had managed to sell 17s 6d worth of raffle tickets, less the cost of the tickets at 1s 3d.

This was enough to get two of us to Exeter station which was at least part way there.

We knew a few players from school but as it was the holidays and we didn't have their phone numbers, we had to cycle round to where we thought they lived and pick up any other players we saw on the way.

That first morning as we rode to Abbotsham some six miles away it felt very much as if we were in the Magnificent Seven, recruiting candidates who could cope with such a tough assignment.

We found our target, Leslie Driftwood, kicking a ball around on the village green. He was a year older than Andrew and me and I had always been impressed with his defensive skills in the school playground.

As we sat astride our bikes on the road overlooking the green Leslie was smashing the ball against the side of the village hall. I turned to Andrew with an enquiring look. He nodded his approval and if he had been smoking would surely have also had a pull on his cheroot before spitting out a long line of orange liquid onto the ground and beating the trail dust out of his cowboy hat.

Boys, unlike girls, rarely waste words and the conversation went something like this:

'Alright Les?'
'Yeah'

'Fancy playing in Europe?'

'OK'

'See you Tuesday on that waste ground at the bottom of Orchard Hill.'

It is a shame some of today's footballers could not take a leaf out of our minimalist transfer negotiations.

Anyhow we were happy, we had our Charles Bronson.

There was another lad, Peter Dark, who lived only half a mile from our little stadium. He was a year younger than Andrew and me and a bit older than Socks. He was one of those poorly boys who could well have turned up in one of those government information films on rickets.

He was always going down with bronchitis and his mother always made him wear a vest and was for ever rubbing some kind of animal fat into his chest. The poor lad smelt like a Christmas turkey but boy could he play.

He was like an electric eel, wriggling and writhing around players at speed. He was a classic winger, lively and full of tricks.

But Peter suffered for his art and after every run down the right wing he turned purple and coughed and spluttered.

The other great thing about Peter was that he had a proper leather football which he treasured and slept with. He always had that ball at his feet going to school, knocking it against walls and trees and running onto the return.

He dribbled around lamp posts and chipped the ball over puddles, a cross between George Best and Tiny Tim.

We rode on our bikes up to his house. Andrew rode a chopper which was all the craze at the time; they were so expensive but his granddad was some bigwig in the local Westminster bank and he gave it to him for his last birthday.

My bike was a customised job, a standard boys' bike which had the mudguards and chain guard removed and replaced with racing ones and a pair of enormous cow-horn handle bars.

We were not quite sure which house Pete lived in on Limers Lane, but as we freewheeled down the slope we spotted a washing line with twelve small vests hanging. All the vests had a transparent patch in the middle from his mother's chest rubs; we were at the right house.

I knocked on the door and Pete opened it. His mum shouted from inside asking him if was wearing his vest as he could catch his death standing in the doorway.

The boy that came to the door looked very much like the boy in the poster on the doctor's surgery wall warning about vitamin D deficiency. He looked a dead cert for a shadow on his lung. I was never quite sure what that meant, but I was always hearing women at bus stops talk about it in hushed voices.

His house was one of those where you never got past the front door. I never saw his father and never asked, but I always heard a man coughing up phlegm every time I called.

His mother was a right old battle-axe who never smiled and I think that is why Peter was so mad for football, despite all his ailments; it got him away from the house.

Pete was keen to join and that made five players. We were on our way.

The next potential player on our radar was a bit of an odd-bod called Johnny Neptune.

His parents were rich and very liberal. His dad was a businessman and flew a lot to the USA. Despite that they were rather like hippies and the rumour was that most weekends there was an orgy going on at chez Neptune.

The family lived in what can only be described as a cross between a giant Swedish log cabin and a smart Swiss skiing chalet. It was the kind of home that shouted Jason King as every room had a shag-pile carpet including the bathroom which also had a bidet.

One teatime when I was at Johnny's, I innocently asked what the bidet was for and Johnny's mother June's graphic, three-minute explanation gave me more knowledge about ladies' plumbing bits than some of the country's leading gynae-cologists could have done.

The bidet part also reinforced the Jason King theory, as I am sure that would have been an essential part of his pad, to ensure that his harem had a respite from his reputation between the purple silk sheets.

Johnny was not a bad player but he got easily distracted. His main interest was dressing up in the weird and wonder-ful outfits his dad brought back from the states.

When you knocked on the door of the house, you never knew who would open the door. One day it would be Troy Tem-pest of *Stingray* and the next Jo Namath, the American football legend.

I guess the clues were there as I heard that many years later he was a member of a Village People tribute band called 'The Hamlet Folk'.

Legend has it that Johnny's parents tragically perished in a fondue accident in the early seventies. The details are sketchy, but at the time I remember over-hearing my parents talking about the accident in hushed tones and I was able to pick out the words, boiling oil, wet fish and kaftans.

Johnny was hired and we had our first striker. My only worry was what costume he would turn up in to a game?

In one of the monster games in the park, a new lad turned up playing in goal between two enormous piles of jumpers and windcheaters. He was called Alan Spring and we immediately gave him the nickname 'Springy'. It seemed to be the vogue then to just add on a 'Y' to the end of anyone's name to come up with a nick-name. We looked around for appreciation at how creative and matey we all were.

Alan had moved down to Devon from his home town of Leicester.

Leicester is a breeding ground for 'keep-ers, with Gordon Banks, England's World Cup winning custodian, and his talented prodigy, Peter Shilton, having played for the local league club.

From that first moment in the park we realised that Springy was special and we had to have him in goal for Redstar United.

He was a natural acrobat and was like a character from a *Boy's Own* comic.

One name that kept cropping up when the talk of recruitment was raised was Stevie Brown. He went to a different school in the town and we had never seen him in the kick-abouts in the park.

Stevie was a football nut who spent every waking hour perfecting his touch by kicking a ball thousands of times against a wall.

We got the address of a disused factory in East-the-water. The next Saturday morning Andrew Cordell and I set out on our bikes, riding along Bideford Quay and crossing the old bridge that spans the Torridge.

Thump, thump, thump, we heard him first before entering a disused warehouse. On the walls in different coloured chalks were drawn various size goals and targets.

The figure before us slammed the ball into the top corner of a chalked goal, controlled the rebounding ball with his chest before flicking it over his shoulder and chipped the ball up, hitting a blue circle high up on the opposite wall.

Steve saw us, went bright red and caught the ball.

'Hi Steve, we have our own team called Redstar United and want you to play for us.'

Stevie went even redder and began to stammer, thought better of it and nodded.

We had heard about the stammer and that it had stopped him getting involved in games with other kids.

He gave us a ten-minute demonstration of what he could do with a ball and Andy and I were both gobsmacked. He could do anything with it and we hoped he could display the same genius out on the pitch.

We now had to fill just three places in the team. A boy called Adrian Small, who was in fact as tall as a house, lived in the same village as Leslie Driftwood.

He was rather unspectacular but could head a ball and was very reliable.

Phil Pocock was in the same year as Andrew and me at school. His claim to fame was that his dad once had a trial for Exeter City. Phil would certainly not be bothering the city scouts, or come to think of it even the local scout team. His football talent lasted about as long as a soluble aspirin. Still he had two feet and had a habit of annoying the opposition by always being in the way, so we found him a place in defence.

The funny thing about Phil was that one year he went on holiday to Spain with his parents and came back with a matador's outfit. Complete with hat, tunic, breeches and cape, it was the genuine article and must have cost a bomb.

Every year at primary school we had a fancy dress competition and Phil always went as a matador.

Everyone else made their own costume so I knew there would be no chance of him winning. That first year a kid went dressed in a sheet with hundreds of seaside postcards stuck to it. Across his forehead in lipstick was written 'A Holiday'. He got a tin of Quality Street for that. I and forty other kids went dressed as cowboys.

I moved away from north Devon when I was thirteen and did not return for another ten years. I was walking down Mill Street late one Saturday evening when a stag party fell out of the pub I was trying to enter.

There at the front was an overweight and very drunk Phil wearing, you guessed it, his matador outfit. The sleeves were halfway up his arms and the short jacket showed a good foot of fat belly. The breeches were now more like incredibly tight shorts. Perched on his head was the tiny matador's hat. He had a little red cape tied around his neck.

I will say one thing about his folks. They knew an investment when they saw it because he didn't half get some wear out of that outfit.

The final piece of our football team jigsaw was Keith King, who lived a couple of doors up from Peter Dart.

Keith was an OK footballer and the happiest person I have ever met.

He was always laughing and smiling. I would even wager that if you tied him to a chair and tortured his pet tortoise in front of him, he would still be chortling away.

Sadly our European dream was over almost before it began.

We were never going to be able to raise enough money and most of the parents were very half-hearted about helping in any effective way. They gave us a little more for pocket money and for washing the car and other chores, but no way was it going to get the pride of north Devon into Europe.

Still we were happy with our little ground, playing small games six v five with all the team. The pitch was just about big enough for these small-sided games, but no way was it big enough for a proper eleven-a-side match.

We borrowed a lawn mower each week to cut the grass and Andy's dad even had a roller, which we all pushed to build our muscles and try and keep the pitch as flat as possible.

We played every day after school when it was lighter and most of Saturday and Sunday. During the school holidays we played all day with little gaps of bike riding and general clowning around.

We had crazes for being different teams and one that lasted most of one summer was St Etienne after Johnny Neptune went to France on holiday.

Our football skills were improving all the time, especially our passing and movement off the ball. Some of the more technically gifted players like Pete Dart and Stevie Brown had amazing dribbling skills. You couldn't coach Pete, everything was instinctive. He just knew what to do and I guess all those hours of being in different situations on the pitch and all the split decisions he had to make made him the terrific player he was.

Those days, weeks and months were the happiest of times. If you could bottle them and keep them with you forever you would be a king.

COMIC RELIEF

The decline in street football has kept pace with the decline in boys' comics so that only the *Beano* and *Dandy* remain from the traditional comics.

Something of a Great British institution that started as far back as 1870, they reached a peak in the decades from 1930 to 1960. There was plenty of football in these comics, notably in *Tiger*, *Wizard* and the *Hotspur*.

Roy of the Rovers

Roy Race was by far the best known comic character and played for the mighty Melchester Rovers. He began his playing career in 1954, playing centre forward alongside his life-long buddy Blackie Gray. Roy became player-manager in the mid-seventies and gave up playing only in 1993 when he had his trusty left foot amputated after a helicopter accident. How much must that have been insured for, the most famous left foot in the world?

To have played at the top flight of football until your late fifties is something that not even the great Stanley Matthews managed.

The famous yellow and red shirts were as famous as Manchester United's or Real Madrid's kit and Roy Race was an ambassador for everything that was right in the game.

No other comic football strip came close to *Roy of the Rovers* for popularity.

Billy's Boots

Billy Dane was a young lad who found a pair of antique football boots while cleaning out his Grandma's loft.

The boots used to belong to legendary centre forward, 'Dead Shot' Keen. Billy was pretty rubbish at football and could not even get into the school team, but once he put on the old pair of boots he was world class. Every other week they were stolen or lost and he would have to play without them, and was usually rubbish, but occasionally good. Was it the boots themselves which gave him the hardest shot in football? And how come he was always in the right place at the right time?

One theory was that Billy was actually a great player and the boots just gave him the confidence he needed to perform. Not sure about that one, but one thing was certain, he had the ageing powers of Cliff Richard. The years rolled on by and he still looked young enough to continue playing for the school team for the next twenty years.

'Dead Shot' Keen had also been a brilliant cricketer and Billy also managed to find a pair of his old cricket boots some years later. The cricket boots seemed to have the same effect as the football boots and turned young master Danes into the next Fred Trueman (Google him if you don't know who he was).

Limp Along Leslie

This was an absolute cracker, about a young sheep farmer called Leslie Tomson, who due to a childhood accident had been left with one leg shorter than the other. Leslie was constantly torn between his love of sheep on his Low Dyke Farm, near the village of Dalestone, in Hilly Peakshire, and football.

He was good enough to play inside left for Darbury Rangers in the top league. Everything came to a head when he was selected to play for England in an international at Hampden Park against Scotland. But it clashed with the National Sheepdog Trial that he had entered with his small black and white sheepdog, Pal.

Leslie's father, the late great John Tomson, was captain of Darbury Rangers and a full England international. He also won an international sheep dog trial with his well known dog, Skipper. What a choice to make. I wonder what John Terry or Wayne Rooney would do in the same circumstances?

It got even better when a local man, Abe Peel, was caught stealing sheep from Leslie's farm and imprisoned. Kind-hearted Leslie promises to look after the thief's two sheepdogs, Ribb and Deacon. When Abe is released he even finds him a job on the farm.

Limp Along Leslie is a belter, a mix of *One Man and his Dog* and *Match of the Day* and tested every possible emotion.

The story appeared in the *Wizard* along with another story called *The Dog with the Yorkshire Accent*. Later comics like *Viz* with strips like *Billy the Fish* parodied the stories found in such comics as *Wizard*, but it was very difficult to come up with any stories as bizarre as some of the supposedly serious strips in the traditional boys' comics.

There Was Once a Game Called Football

In the year 2148, schoolboys Phil Mason and Lawrie Hill, of Coventry, are working on a history project together on old games and pastimes. They come across the ancient game of association football and are intrigued.

The boys represent the school at the sport of Riposta, which is a game played with long-handled rackets on a big concrete court. You scored when the ball hit targets at either end of the court and flashed up on a big electronic scoreboard.

Phil becomes more and more interested in this strange game of football and even manufactures a ball from a light metal called Baronium, to which he fits a valve and fills with Ultrahelium gas.

He gets school teams together, but the sports teacher catches them playing and shouts: 'What is this tomfoolery?'

Then it appears to all boil down to whether you prefer to play Riposta or footie? Phil and Lawrie are dead keen to spread the game far afield as had been done many generations before.

Other comic stories

Other football strips included *Bobby of the Blues*, *Nipper*, the story of Nipper Lawrence, a young orphan lad who played for Blackport Rovers. As Blackport Rovers suggests, the writers were not that creative when making up team names.

They appeared to just take the professional league club names, cut them in half and draw them out of a hat. You then came up with names such as Everpool and Liverton.

More football comic characters were Johnny Dexter, a tough tackling, uncompromising centre half, who appeared in the strip *The Hard Man.* Gordon Stewart was the young Scottish goalkeeper in *The Safest Hands in Soccer.* Now that was real fiction at its best!

Another comic strip about a 'keeper appeared in the *Wizard* under the title, *Bernard Briggs.* Bernard is also orphaned at a young age and has his own scrap business in the town of Slagton. He rides around on a motorcycle and sidecar which he has made from an old bath tub.

Every week he tries a new sport and is sensational at them all. As well as being a brilliant goalie, he is also fantastic at Baseball, Boxing, Rugby League, Ice Hockey, Tennis and Wrestling.

Then there was *Gorgeous Gus*, the story of a wealthy, upper-class footballer who had his own private dressing-room, creased shorts and a valet to dress him.

Other strips were, *Tommy's Troubles*, about a lad who wants to play football at a rugby-playing school. Then there was *Durrell's Palace, Wayne's Wolves, Playmaker, Hotshot Hamish and Mighty Mouse, The Footballer Who Wouldn't Stay Dead, Future Ball, Dream 'keeper, Goalmouth, Kevin's Chance, The Wheelchair Wonder* and a strip about a boy with a table football team called *Mike's Mini Men*.

TOTAL FOOTBALL – THE DUTCH & OTHERS

> *We must free our soccer youth
> from the shackles of playing
> to order, along rails as it were.
> We must give them ideas and
> encourage them to develop
> their own.*
>
> **Willy Meisl**

As a seventeen-year-old in 1974 I was still grieving over England's elimination at the qualifying stage of the World Cup and that damn clown in the Polish goal, to really be that bothered about the 1974 World Cup finals.

That all changed when I began to watch the Dutch. I wanted a Dutch shirt and to look like Ruud Krol. The football they played was in a new dimension and you knew that you were watching something very special unfold before you.

The pundits called it Dutch Total Football and I loved it.

I became besotted with all things Dutch and sat glued to the screen during the duration of the World Cup in West Germany.

That's how I wanted to play football and I became really interested in tactics and how teams played. The World Cup panel on TV were really interesting, talking about the way teams played and going into depth.

The roots of Total Football were born many years before when an Austrian sports writer by the name of Willy Meisl described a method of play he called 'the whirl', a fluid system with players interchanging positions on the pitch.

He wrote about his older brother Hugo's Austrian 'Wunderteam' of the 1930s, predicting in his book *Soccer Revolution*, written in 1955, that this would be the way teams would play in the future.

The 1950s Hungarian team, the Mighty Magyars, led by Puskas, played a style of

Total Football with Hidegkuti playing as a deep lying centre forward, a role that Cruyff would play twenty years later for Ajax and Holland.

We associate the Dutch with Total Football although even then there is a debate about who instigated it? Some even suggest it was an Englishman, Vic Buckingham who arrived as Ajax coach in 1959.

He was previously manager at West Bromwich Albion and got his team to move around the pitch, encouraging his fullbacks to overlap the wingers. Up till then it was very unusual for them to cross the halfway line without a passport.

The great coach Don Howe was one of those fullbacks and when he skipped down the wing past the winger, the Hawthorns fans near him would enquire. 'What the **** are you doing here?'

Recognition in the main has centred on three candidates, coach Rinus Michels, Cruyff and the unlikely Velibor Vasovic, the Serbian sweeper at Ajax under Michels.

Years later I came across David Winner's superb book *Brilliant Orange*. He argues the fact, supported by many Dutch coaches I have spoken to, that Vasovic began to bring the ball out of defence and wave a player into his position and so on.

German legend, and another sweeper who could bring the ball from defence, Franz Beckenbauer, is sceptical that it was a planned way of playing.

'It owed more to the element of surprise than to any magic formula,' he said. 'I think the Dutch got away with it for so long because the opposition could not work out what tactics they were facing.

'It never dawned on them, certainly not until it was too late, that there were no tactics at all,' Beckenbauer said. 'Just brilliant players with a ball.'

So did Total Football really come from the streets of Amsterdam, Rotterdam, Utrecht and later from Surinam in the Dutch East Indies? Is this not the breeding ground for intelligent, creative players worldwide?

The key was that although Michels worked them very hard in training, he gave them the freedom on the pitch to express themselves and be creative.

So the kind of football we played all those years ago, practising our skills and heaps of trial and error was a great way to learn the game.

My love affair with the Dutch game continues today and I go there every year with coaches to see what they are doing in football and to talk for hours and hours with the older guys about Ajax, Cruyff, 1974 and Total Football.

A BREAK FOR CRICKET

*Asif Masood, the Pakistani
fast bowler, who approaches
the wicket like Groucho Marx
chasing a pretty waitress ...*
John Arlott

During those long hot summer holidays
when our football friends were away and
we could not summon the strength to
cycle to the park for a game, my brother
and I used our imaginations to conjure up
a whole Test series that involved twenty-
two cricketers but was played by just two
boys in a sloping garden. We spent days
playing and it was always the Ashes series
in the summer of 1968.

I was England, my brother Australia.

We would go through all four innings
and if I went into bat first I was the following England team: JH Edrich, G Boycott, KF
Barrington, TW Graveney, MC Cowdrey*,

BL D'Oliveira, APE Knott, R Illingworth, JA Snow, K Higgs, DL Underwood.

We only had one set of stumps so I would start off as John Edrich, batting left-handed, with the invisible Geoff Boycott at the other end. If I scored one run, remembering to shout out 'in' at the top of my voice as I crossed the crease, I would then walk back to the stumps end and bat right handed as Geoff Boycott.

We would even copy their mannerisms and style of play. So when I was Geoff Boycott I would be very defensive and when I was Ken Barrington try and hook everything for four.

When we played football and were running down the wing before shooting at goal we would commentate things like, 'That's not so very far away' in a mock Kenneth Wolstenholme voice as you flashed one just past the left-hand jumper.

In cricket we were always the wonderful John Arlott, which was a lot more difficult as you had to be much more eloquent with your adjectives.

My brother kept all the records of the games in one of those brilliant little pocket scorebooks. He wrote everything in pencil so we could re-use the book time and time again with games in the garden, and with the indoor game of 'Owzat'.

As my brother was always Australia he fielded the following team: WM Lawry*, IR Redpath, RM Cowper, KD Walters, AP Sheahan, IM Chappell, BN Jarman, NJN Hawke, GD McKenzie, JW Gleeson, AN Connolly.

He would start with two fast bowlers and then change to another bowler. To make it as accurate as possible you had to copy the bowler's run up and action and bowl left-handed if need be.

The one that had me in fits of giggles was when my brother was Jackie Gleeson, the spin bowler. He was always chewing gum and pulling a face which he replicated brilliantly, although his spin bowling was pretty atrocious and I was able to get most of my runs off him.

The ten fielders were as follows:

The wicketkeeper was a garden chair and the three slips were jumpers laid out on the grass with the arms spread so as to optimise catches.

Gully was a bush, and square leg a small tree. Silly mid-off was another spread out jumper and long-off and long-on were a tree and a telegraph pole. That left third-man which was another garden chair.

If you nicked the ball and then it hit a tree, chair or landed on a jumper you were out caught. As in the proper game, it mustn't hit the ground first, but for nine, ten, jack we made a rule up that the ball after being hit needed only to hit a tree or a jumper to be out caught, even if it had travelled all the way along the ground.

We had an agreed boundary which involved hedges and other borders, and, of course, if it went out of the garden it was the time honoured, 'six and out'.

When it came for my turn to bowl, I loved being Ken Higgs who stuck out his bum and ran in a most peculiar manner. That one always had my brother in hysterics.

The other two I loved to imitate was my hero, fast bowler John Snow, and the spin of Ray Illingworth.

Looking back, the imagination and eye for detail was incredible. Cricket with just two of you is not the easiest of games to play because you are forever chasing a ball, but with fielders and lots of possibilities of catches from the static fielders the game came alive.

The main disputes came with lbw appeals and as I touched on earlier, not saying 'in' after taking a run.

To spice up the action we sometimes did tip and run where you had to make a run after hitting the ball. This usually came about after I had been Geoff Boycott for a whole morning and scored only six runs.

Cricket ran football a close second in our affections and we would also play with most of the football crowd down the park during the summer.

The other favourite was playing cricket down at Northam burrows. When the wind was not too strong we played on the beach, but otherwise we played on the other side of the steep bank of pebbles and out of the wind on an area of sand and scrub.

This became a birthday treat for some of the local children with a couple of dads organising the cricket while the mums laid out a picnic of egg, sardine and Sandwich Spread sandwiches, crisps, cake and Tizer.

INDOOR PURSUITS

Computers have been blamed in today's society for keeping children in solitary confinement and denying them the great outdoors and all its wonderful benefits.

There was also a dark force back in the sixties that threatened to stunt the growth of tens of thousands of boys and keep them from sunlight for days on end.

Boys would eventually emerge from the darkness; starving hungry, dehydrated, with skin the colour of uncooked pastry and bloodshot eyes after a monumental inter-street Subbuteo competition.

The World Cup, FA Cup and even the occasional Fairs Cup were played out on bedroom floors and dining room tables from Dartmouth to Durham, fought out between boys with uneven fringes and strained index fingers.

Subbuteo had the effect of a class A drug; it hooked us completely and without warning.

My brother got a starter set for his birthday, two teams, one red, one blue, a pitch and a couple of balls.

We played for hours and pored over the Subbuteo catalogue to see what other teams and accessories were available. Television crews, floodlights, stands and spectators, you could get the lot, and we worked feverishly on paper rounds and car washing to save up for our new found craze.

I spent hours making stands and terraces from wood, and cut out adverts from magazines and newspapers to stick on them. As well as buying the Subbuteo spectators, who were decked out with scarves and rattles, I bought the little figures you could get with train sets, guards, passengers and farm workers.

The only problem was half the crowd were carrying milk churns and hay bales. The kids who played Subbuteo a decade later could make it even more authentic and give them names such as the 'milk churn crew' or the 'hay bale casuals' and have them attack rival groups of supporters by hitting them over the head with their churns or drown them in milk and give them a nasty allergic rash from the hay.

Subbuteo was not without its problems, and some of the arguments could be even more intense than the real thing.

The biggest fights came over how you moved the player on the ball. The correct way was to flick your index finger at the base of the player and not use your thumb for extra leverage in the manner of flicking a piece of snot from the sleeve of your school blazer.

Using your thumb was illegal, but many players persisted with this technique, especially when shooting on goal.

The worst flicking technique came from one of my brother's friends. Tim, was a lovely lad, and no mean footballer, until you played him at Subbuteo.

He would do a sideways karate chop across the pitch which not only played the ball forward but at the same time moved five of his players into attacking positions and scattered your midfield to the four corners of the globe.

This Hong Kong Phooey approach to table football was plain cheating and the rows that developed threatened many friendships.

The other potentially explosive problem was goalkeepers, and moving goals, especially at penalties.

When the opposing player was taking a shot you were meant to hold the goal with one hand and the goalkeeper stand with the other, but alas many didn't.

When player A took a shot to the goal-keeper's right, player B would jerk his 'keeper to the right taking the goal with it towards the corner flag leaving the ball to trickle over the line where the goal had once stood.

'Missed' would be the gleeful shout of your opponent as you threw yourself across the table to land a punch anywhere you could. The rage burned deep because of the way some cheats conducted themselves on the Subbuteo pitch.

We refereed our own games in the park and we were always able to sort out any problems or disputes, but Subbuteo was different.

My brother is a lovely chap and we never had fights until we both got infected by the table football bug.

My brother was a fanatic and would play the whole FA Cup on the dining room table. Thirty-two teams playing ninety-minute matches with extra time if needed. Mainly he played this by himself, noting down all the fixtures, teams, results, scorers and attendances in an exercise book. He spent hours playing and commentating though every minute of every game.

I sometimes played with him, until that fateful afternoon when Fulham entertained Plymouth Argyle in the quarter-final.

The score was one all going into the last minute and I was desperate for a win. Then I made the cardinal sin from a goal kick of just smashing the ball forward, flicking 'bogie away' style. The ball travelled up the pitch, hit his 'keeper before he had a chance to move him and the ball deflected into the goal. I jumped up to celebrate and he whacked me.

Over the intervening years, at family christenings, weddings and funerals, I look into my brother's eyes to explore deep down and past the smile to see if he has forgiven me. All I ever see is a large white plastic ball ricochet off the yellow-shirted 'keeper, moulded into a permanent dive, and trickle into the back of the net. The forty-plus years of raw hurt is still there.

THE DUMP GANG

In our search for a proper game against good opposition, Redstar's attention turned towards the Dump Gang.

They were a group of boys aged between twelve and fourteen who struck fear into the rest of the town's children.

They were worse than the bogey man because they were made of flesh and blood and lived in our street.

They were the cause of many nightmares, and if you had been discussing one of their alleged atrocities during the day and combined that with a midnight feast of a Jacob's Cream Cracker and a generous hunk of cheddar, you had the potential to outdo the worst acid trip imaginable.

One positive outcome of the Dump Gang's reign of terror was the number of outstanding middle-distance runners who came out of north Devon in the 1970s. This was because a whole generation of boys had been running home from cubs and brass band practice on dark, windy nights in near Olympic qualifying times, which is not bad for children under ten years of age.

Every shadow on every street was a possible member of the Dump Gang so you had to travel fast.

The name of the Dump Gang was very appropriate as the tiny local M&S store had a larger volume of sales of boys' underpants than the flagship store on Oxford Street.

The local M&S staff had big bonuses every year and most could afford a good family holiday off the back of it, so the Dump Gang's influence spread much further than they would ever realise.

M&S spent years trying to decipher the 'north Devon boys' pants phenomena', hoping they could replicate the same level of sales elsewhere, but could never fathom the most unusual buying trend.

It was testimony to the company that their pants were purchased by worried mothers for their 'follow through' capabilities, but this was not the same reason given by the mums when questioned by the bright young things from marketing who had travelled down from London for the week to get some hard evidence. But the evidence was anything but hard as the poor overworked mums found to their cost every washday Monday.

They were actually called the Dump Gang because their headquarters was a small collection of derelict farm buildings on waste ground next to the town's rubbish dump.

I once visited their HQ with my older brother and his friend and I have never been so scared in my life.

Luckily the buildings were deserted, but the stories I heard on that trip sent a chill deep down into my soul. I was not certain if the dark brown stains on the corrugated walls were blood or rust.

Once they locked Kevin Smedley in the old outside lav they used as a jail for two hours. This meant Kevin missed his tea which was probably the worst thing that could happen to a child in those days.

You could do what you wanted in the day, travel to Timbuktu and back, build a nuclear submarine or swim across crocodile infested rivers, as long as you were home in time for tea.

The boiled egg must have been going hard, the jam sandwiches curling and the tea stewing and growing cold, despite the quilted tea cosy that had the heat saving properties of a Special Forces sleeping bag.

I watched the main BBC TV news and could not understand that such a serious criminal act was not reported.

Another story that had done the rounds and had added to the gang's terrifying but legendary status was that they had once killed a cat.

The most chilling version I had heard was that it was the vicar's cat, which added a satanic thread to their murderous antics.

This was also when I learned that cats do indeed have nine lives as different stories included the cat being drowned in the font, being flung from the church tower, strangled with the bell rope and force fed communion wine before being strapped to a home made go-kart and pushed down the steepest hill in the town.

The last grizzly feline death was witnessed by the vicar's unfortunate wife and her two young traumatised children.

They saw their drunken, prize-winning Siamese hurtling downwards on a collision course with the no. 38 bus to Barnstaple. An old-aged pensioner on the other side of the road swore blind that the pampered moggy was singing the first few bars of 'My Way' as he flew past.

The reputation of the Dump Gang grew and grew, but although I know poor Kevin Smedley's abduction to be true, I expect the nearest they got to cruelty to cats was throwing the occasional stone at a stray.

It seemed that we were taking on a huge task for our first game as these boys were a cross between Real Madrid and the Krays but to be successful in Europe we needed a challenge.

It was left to me and Andy to seek out the Dump Gang and arrange a match. Walking to their headquarters my mind began to wander and I thought of all the possible tortures that might await me. The one that really haunted me was having my genitals tied up with barbed wire while they force-fed me the skin off the top of the custard.

The meeting was brief and not nearly as bad as we had imagined. I came away with my genitals intact and our very first fixture: Redstar United v the Dump Gang at Westward Ho! beach arranged for a week's time.

That day the Redstar United team met up outside the Quay Gift shop, mounted their bikes and began the four-mile journey to the beach.

We looked good all cycling together and I grew more confident as the excited shouts and chatter increased with each mile.

We took the short cut to Westward Ho!, along the narrow road through the golf course and to the large pebble ridge where we left our bikes.

We spent a long time preparing the pitch in the firm sand so that it looked as perfect as the one at Wembley Stadium and began a kick-about to try and calm our nerves for the big match ahead. After a few minutes we became hot and stripped off our jumpers.

I had asked the team to get their mums to sew a red star onto a T-shirt so that we looked like a proper team. What I hadn't told them was the size and how many points it should have.

When everyone lined up to do a pretend meet the Queen and head of FIFA I was shocked.

Andrew had a tiny star with five points on the left of his chest, just above his heart while Johnny Neptune had a massive star with many points that went from his navel all the way up to just under his chin. Everyone had a different slant on a red star. Some were on the left, others on the right and a few in the middle. There were all shades of red from virtually orange to a maroon red colour. What a disaster!

Then Peter shouted for us all to listen, and then we heard the sound of a horde of people walking up the steep bank of pebbles. We could not see anyone at this point, then with the sun shining behind them we saw the silhouettes of figures carrying spears. The film *Zulu* had recently been on at the cinema, which everyone had watched and talked about for weeks. For the boys on that lonely beach, the Battle of Rorke's Drift was about to be relived.

We were all frozen in terror and a pool of water began to form at Socks' feet as he wet himself in sheer fright. One poor lad broke wind and later we saw him sobbing, gingerly walking towards his bike and realised that he had followed through and was out of the game. The only saving grace was that for once he was not wearing his matador outfit. The squelching sound as he sat on the saddle was a noise I didn't want to hear again, but sadly did from my own saddle a few years later after my first cider drinking escapade.

Where were Bromhead, Chard, Hook and the other heroes of Rorke's Drift when you needed them?

The silhouettes were not, of course, Zulus and the spears were, in fact, garden canes the Dump Gang had bought for the goalposts, and corner flags, but young boys' vivid imaginations had been working overtime. The advantage had been given to the Dump Gang before a ball had even been kicked.

The Redstar United team that memorable day, playing in an England World Cup winning 4-3-3 formation, was: Alan Spring (goalkeeper), Phil Pocock (right back), Jonathon Cordell, 'Socks', (left back), Leslie Driftwood (centre half), Adrian Small (centre half), Keith King (midfield), Paul 'me' (midfield), Andrew Cordell (midfield), Pete Dart (forward/winger), Stevie Brown (forward), Johnny Neptune (forward).

We were determined to make the game special and we all lined up as they do before the FA Cup final and international matches.

We shook hands and Socks let out a yell. 'He's just done a Chinese Burn on me'.

The Dump Gang captain argued that they should have both choice of which way they were kicking, towards the dead dogfish end, and kick-off.

From the start, their centre forward touched the ball forward to the player they called 'Hatchet Harry' and he blasted the ball towards our goal. Our 'keeper, Alan Spring, saw it late but flung himself to his right and at full stretch tipped the ball around the post.

The ball was then caught by the stiff breeze and began to race across the sand. Socks gave chase, head up looking at the sky and arms pumping with his hands in karate chop mode.

The ball whizzed past the dead dogfish and various other bits of flotsam and jetsam, before hitting a courting couple kissing on the beach.

'Bugger off four eyes!' said the boyfriend.

'Same to you with knobs on,' said Socks.

From the goal kick, Alan Spring kicked the ball short to Phil Pocock at right back and he passed to me in the centre before I played it back towards the right wing and Pete Dart.

Before Pete had a chance to touch it, he was flattened by the in-rushing Hatchet Harry. 'Foul,' we shouted in unison.

Andrew and I picked up the limp winger who was gasping for breath.

'I'm winded' he murmured, holding back the tears.

A couple of minutes later the Dump Gang opened the scoring when a lad with a face like the moon slotted home from close range after a raid down the left wing.

Hatchet Harry added a second a minute later with a thunderbolt from outside the area. Their third was a bizarre own goal when a Leslie Driftwood clearance found the back of Sock's head – the ball looped up and over the head of Alan Spring and into the goal.

Andrew shouted at his younger brother and Socks told him he had a 'black soul' and left the pitch for ten minutes in a sulk to play with the dead dogfish.

If we didn't get our act together we were in for a thumping. The ball was fed out on the right to little Peter Dart; Hatchet Harry came steaming in but Pete deftly dragged the ball back with the sole of his foot and the big oaf, still motoring, stumbled forward and fell face down into the sand. Pete moved forward and knocked the ball around the outside of the next challenge before running around the other side to meet the ball. He cut inside the next player and slipped the ball to Johnny Neptune on the left who thumped the ball past the advancing 'keeper.

Redstar United had just scored their first ever goal and what a cracker it was.

We were now flying and playing some good football. Alan Spring was making acrobatic saves in goal and Keith King, Andrew and I were passing the ball well while our forwards looked lively. Pete Dart was beginning to take them apart with his mesmerising play on both wings.

As the game progressed we became more confident and the Dump Gang grew more frustrated. However, not all the Redstar players were playing at their maximum – Socks spent most of the time hopping from one foot to the other while trying to keep himself as far away from the action and the ball as possible.

Our second goal was a gem. Alan Spring took a quick short goal kick to Adrian Small who passed the ball to Keith King in midfield. He played a quick one-two with me before knocking it forward to Stevie Brown. Stevie turned sharply and shaped to smash the ball before deftly chipping it past the 'keeper as he came out.

We pressed forward looking for the equaliser and Andrew played a peach of a ball at Pete's feet. The nifty winger skipped around a challenge and cut in on goal. He was just about to pull the trigger when he was sandwiched by Hatchet Harry and a gangly boy they called Lurch.

You could hear the air leaving his lungs as he fell to the floor convulsing and shaking. His concerned team-mates gathered round and Andy lifted up Pete's shirt and gasped. 'He's not wearing a vest!' he exclaimed, which made everyone worry twice as much. As far as we knew, other than when he was having the weekly bath, he had always worn a vest because of all his respiratory problems.

By this time the Dump Gang had wandered off and the game was over.

Socks was sent to get help and we saw him race towards the café at the end of the beach, wiping tears and snot away with the back of his hand. He splashed through the large pools of water that were beginning to form with the incoming tide.

Andrew's and Socks's granddad drove down in his Austin 40 and Pete was carried to the car and put on the back seat.

It was a few weeks before we saw him when we played a proper team on a proper pitch. Redstar United's reputation was growing.

NORTON BOYS

It was funny how some games got arranged. It always seemed to be, second, third or fourth hand from a friend of a friend's cousin.

When Leslie Driftwood came over to my house to play a Subbuteo Fairs Cup final second leg, he casually mentioned that he had arranged a game with the mighty Norton Boys.

They were the only proper team that I knew of who played on the same pitch as the men's team, complete with changing rooms, proper goals, nets and even corner flags.

The only time we had ever had a chance to shoot into a proper goal with nets was for twelve seconds at the Sports Ground before the killjoy groundsman threw us off.

Norton Boys even had their own kit of which we were in awe. A smart blue round-neck shirt, blue shorts and red stockings.

As we all cycled to their pitch I was expecting to be disappointed and find that the game was a hoax. But as we entered the gates their players were putting up the nets and the butterflies in my stomach did several loop the loops.

A man wearing a smart royal blue tracksuit greeted us and showed us to our dressing-room. He was the boys' coach who even took them for a weekly training session. We could only ever dream of such a thing.

Looking around the room I was confident that we could put on a display and surprise them with our skill.

We put on our boots in silence, each of us contemplating the match ahead.

The pitch was freshly marked out with penalty boxes and semi-circles and I thought I was going to pass out with the excitement. I had to keep pinching myself to make sure this wasn't just one big wonderful dream.

One slight blemish was that the pitch was covered in cow pats. The summer sun had given them a crusty top but as we were later to find they were anything but crusty underneath.

Pete should have no problem we joked, using his terrific dribbling skills to avoid them.

He had recovered from the debacle on the beach and lifted his Redstar shirt to reveal he was wearing two vests, which was a compromise he'd had to agree with for his mother to let him play the match.

Their coach was going to referee the game, another first for most of us.

The opposition team looked very useful and we knew their number nine, Billy Dean, had a reputation in the town for being a fine footballer but also an incredible bighead.

We lined up and straight from the kick-off Norton's centre forward raced up field; the ball was touched back to their skipper, a lad in the year above us called Tony Dicks, who knocked it long down the middle for it to be met by Billy Dean's right boot and we were already 1-0 down.

Was this going to be a thrashing?

Their second followed a couple of minutes later. They were so quick and we just didn't have time to settle and play. We just couldn't think quickly enough and a few minutes later Billy Dean was celebrating his hat-trick.

By half-time we managed to keep the score down to 3-0 with some heroic defending from Leslie Driftwood and Adrian Small, who threw their bodies at everything, and the agility of Alan Spring between the posts. We were thoroughly drained but all agreed we had to try and pass the ball more in the second half and make sure we got Pete Dart involved more in the game.

The turning point came early in the second period when Billy Dean and Adrian Small tussled for a ball in our penalty box. As they went shoulder to shoulder their centre forward stumbled and fell head first into a cowpat – splat!

He was covered, his hair, face, shirt and arms. He stood up in complete shock and disbelief. It took a full thirty seconds for him to understand the enormity of the situation, he spread his arms out, looked up into the sky and howled. It was perhaps the very first time in Association Football that a substitution had to be made because a player was covered from head to toe in cow excrement.

We took the initiative from then on – they were not the same side without their talismanic striker.

Their tempo slackened and we were at them for the rest of the half.

Johnny Neptune pulled a goal back when he tapped in a Pete Dart cross and Steve Brown added a second with a volley into the top corner after Keith King lobbed the ball over their static defence. Even Phil Pocock got on the score sheet when a corner was cleared by their defender who smacked it straight against our right back's nose from which it rebounded into their goal.

I have never seen anyone with a nose-bleed grin so much. He had to go off for the rest of the match and sit with his head between his knees and half a toilet roll stuck up each nostril.

We scored another three goals, the best of which was Pete's in the dying minutes, when he went on a mazy run from the halfway line before tucking the ball into the net.

It is so difficult to put into words how we felt on that hot evening.

Whatever happens in life, whenever you bring such wonderful memories to the surface, a huge grin spreads across your face and you start to laugh at just how brilliant it all was.

KIDS' FOOTBALL TODAY

If children don't play, their minds don't grow. Play is where they learn to make their own decisions, trust their own judgement, set their own targets. It's where they learn to get along with other kids, meet triumph and disaster, and then come home for tea. Adults can help by helping them find somewhere to play, sorting out the boundaries, being handy with the plasters if something goes wrong. But otherwise we should leave them to it!

Sue Palmer
author of *21st Century Boys* and *Toxic Childhood*

I am a fully paid up member of the 'well, in my day we…' club.

It was the one thing I vowed not to do, but here I sit in my cardigan and slippers and bore everyone to death.

I have become a pompous, droning grumpy old man.

Over the years I am sure I have become prone to exaggeration and thinking that things were much better than they actually were.

But the children's game we played in the playground, street and park is a million miles from the adult controlled game that has taken its place.

I had no problem with my dad or grand-dad joining in occasionally or showing me things like how to bowl a googly in cricket. But adults and parents are so much part of children's sport and play-time now it's like your dad coming along on your first date at sixteen or going with you to a Who concert, standing next to you swigging from a can of Colt 45 and remarking, 'Townsend's on fire tonight and Keith is blinding on drums.'

There needs to be a bit of a gap, as there are loads of things we would want to do away from our parents. We were left to get on with it which was great.

I have been involved as a grass-roots football coach for thirteen years and although there are plenty of good things, I have also seen plenty to make me weep.

Kids are not allowed to just roam as we did, and every possible risk appears to have been eliminated from every situation.

The kids now play in leagues from the age of six. They are told to stay in defence and 'hold your position' as well as 'don't dribble it there!'

They have kits with 'Dave & Kens Motors' emblazoned on their shirts, tracksuits, under shirts, drill tops, proper goals, referees and pitches. No room for imagination and dreaming of your first time in a proper kit or shooting into a goal with a net, they get it all in one package at six, the Premier League for tots.

The one thing they can't do is just go outside, put some jumpers down and play a game with their mates. They can't do that now and that is the saddest thing ever.

Substitutes! Who was ever a sub down the park or in the school playground?

How is a six-year-old meant to fall in love with the game when he's standing on the side on a freezing cold January morning, hoping to get on for the last two or three minutes?

Games of ten, twenty goals to nil as coaches feed their own egos. I watched part of one game and asked the coach of an under-tens team why he had not swapped players around or given some to the opposition after a 25-1 win.

He explained that goal difference could be crucial at the end of the season and then turned away and blasted his team for conceding a goal.

We would never allow that. It was not a perfect world by any means but we were very competitive and fair.

In the big games down the park it was usually the older and best footballers who were captains. As they went down the line picking their players in turn, you got two roughly even teams and everyone played. That made it more fun and more competitive. And if one team was, say, winning by five goals to nil, you stopped the game, swapped over a couple of players and started back at 0-0.

All the great players from the past, who have lit up this beautiful game, learned on the streets and were not coached until later when they already had years of trying things, experimenting, decision-making, playing on different surfaces with everything from one-a-side to twenty-a-side, with a variety of balls, playing against kids of different ages and abilities and most important of all, having fun and learning about life.

Not a bad way to grow up.

The quotes in the book were taken from:

Bobby Charlton – *The Book of Football Quotations*, Phil Shaw, Ebury Press and *Sir Bobby Charlton – The Autobiography The Manchester United Years*, Headline.

Jimmy Greaves – *Greavsie*, Time Warner.

Stanley Matthews – *The Way it Was*, Headline Publishing Group.

Paulo de Canio – *The Autobiography*, Harper Collins Willow.

Tom Finney – *My Autobiography*, Headline.

Nobby Stiles – *After the Ball*, Hodder & Stoughton.

George Best – *Blessed*, Ebury Press.

David Ginola – *Le Magnifique*, HarperCollins Willow.

John Arlott – BBC Radio *Test Match Special*.

Ferenc Puskas – *Puskas on Puskas*, Robson Books.